"Downtown White Police is an important book. But above all, it is the most interesting book at the intersection of race and crime that has been published in many years"

-Colin Flaherty, author of "White Girl Bleed A Lot" and
"Don't Make the Black Kids Angry"

"Downtown White Police"

"Downtown White Police"

Demonizing the Alpha Cop, Glorifying Thugs, and Militarizing Law Enforcement

James Lancia

ISBN: 1514288885
ISBN 13: 9781514288887

DEDICATION

To all my brothers in blue who patrolled the dangerous streets of the city at my side.
We engaged the worst of the worst and we overpowered them. We had each other's backs and
we would have given our lives for each other. We are a vanishing breed of men, the last Centurions.

CONTENTS

INTRODUCTION

The greatest threat to the safety of the American citizen today is not an overseas enemy in the guise of terrorism. It is the criminal on the street. These are the ones who rob your possessions, assault your person, invade your home at night and in the day, and kill you. Is there a greater threat anywhere in this country? Walking out of your door puts you at risk every single day, and the cop on the beat is the only protection you have other than what you can do for yourself. The military will not protect you. Your elected political officials will not protect you. As much as police are the target of hatred and mistrust today, you still call them when you need them and you still hope they will come to your rescue in times of trouble. In this book I discuss why the Alpha cop is demonized, why thugs are inexcusably glorified, and why the militarization of police is imminent and not something we should ever accept or allow.

The love/hate relationship between the public and the police is nothing new, but for the past forty or so years, race has played a major role in further straining an already tenuous situation in America. At no other time in history has the public and media sympathized with and glorified violent thugs while turning a blind eye to their criminal actions. Because this is happening now more than ever before, law enforcement is changing, and it is not a change for the better. It is a reaction to a situation that has been allowed to become out of control. Eventually, all law abiding citizens will be affected by the militarization of our police. The fundamental role of the police officer has shifted in part to an occupying army mentality on one hand, and an almost nonexistent or impotent presence on the other. Neither is good for the public. What was once considered "normal police duties" are now being handled by heavily armed and armored tactical units, while regular cops are becoming relegated to the lesser duties of policing. Regular cops seem to be unable to handle the violent thug mentality that is now dominating the streets. Most cops seem to be intimidated by thugs and/or are afraid of the political and public backlash when confronting them. This is a recipe for disaster, and should never dictate how a police officer performs his duties.

The definition of an Alpha Cop for this book is a law enforcement officer that most people would view as the ideal. He is strong, confident, capable, mindful of civil and human rights, and ready to handle any situation. He is not afraid or influenced by public pressures and he knows what his duty is and he does it. They are now a dying breed due to reduced hiring standards, training, and the changing views of police towards a more hostile public. These Alpha Cops are now being demonized by the media and by the indoctrinated and brainwashed public who are constantly influenced by political and social rhetoric. These same entities falsely define the Alpha Cop as a rogue, anachronistic white male who is insensitive and brutish and who is ready to violate anyone's civil rights, but especially the civil rights of a minority. To them he is quick to shoot, profiles people of color, and is inhuman when dealing with the criminal element. This is not only false and misleading, but is debasing to the very fabric of what keeps the streets from getting out of control and subsequently places the law abiding public at risk. There are good cops, average cops, bad cops, corrupt cops, lazy cops, and "do nothings." Then there is the Alpha Cop who is the ideal of what a police officer is expected to be.

Thugs come in all colors. Whether they are members of gangs, groups of homegrown criminals rampaging in our cities and towns, illegal criminal immigrants, or just your run of the mill punk criminal, they terrorize and criminalize our streets. They are oppressors and they severely degrade the quality of life for the rest of us. "Thug" can also be used for a bad and corrupt cop who abuses his authority and the trust that come with the badge. These give the rest of the good, hard working and honest cops a bad name.

In this book I reveal through actual true events, statistics, expert analysis, and scathing honesty an Alpha Cop in action who had his boots on the ground during the most violent years in this country.

* * *

When I was a rookie in 1978 I asked one of my first partners why he became a cop.
He was a Vietnam War Veteran and had experienced heavy combat.
He told me, "Being a cop is the closest thing I could find to warfare."
Wars are fought on many fronts.

* * *

CHAPTER 1

THE CHOICE TO LIVE OR DIE

Today the use of force by police is at the center of many major issues concerning Americans. There are both facts and fiction regarding the lethal force used by law enforcement. Firstly, I would like to dispel the falsity that blacks are targeted by white police officers. More whites are killed by police of all colors than blacks or Hispanics[i] even though statistically, blacks and Hispanics commit more violent crime and engage police officers more often than whites.[ii] In fact, police shootings of blacks are at a 75 year low and down 50%.[iii] Even so, the media, which seem to be complicit in an overall agenda of pitting the public against the police, are ignorant, blind, or willful in perpetuating and maintaining a dangerous myth that the big bad white cop is out to get any black or minority, innocent or guilty. Wrong again.

"Red 42- Priority!"

"42's on. Martin Luther King Drive."

"42. Reports of shots fired from a third floor apartment window. Suspect is a black male with a shotgun. Father Panik Village, building 26, third floor, unable to give you an apartment. Use caution, I'll get you backup."

"42. Responding."

"41. Permission to cover 42."

"10-4; thank you 41. Use a code." 'Code' is the radio call for Lights and Sirens.

"42's on scene. Large crowd outside. Stand by."

Father Panik Village consisted of nearly fifty brick buildings and was the sixth largest housing project in the nation. This infamous place was featured in a New York Times article as the worst public housing project in the United States according to FBI statistics.[iv] It was notorious for crime and was the perfect picture of an urban catastrophe. Father Panik was home to predominately black and Hispanic residents, and although police were a constant sight there, a white face was still an anomaly.

In the Bridgeport Police Department, the sectors of the city were divided by color codes and vehicle numbers. My police unit, Red 42, was a lower East Side patrol car and Father Panik Village was within and part of this sector. Red was a fitting color for this high crime area.

There was a large crowd that had gathered outside the building where the shooter had fired his shotgun at bystanders before our arrival. After scattering to escape the shots that were fired, the crowd returned when they saw our police car pull up to the scene. As we exited our cruiser with our guns in hand, we heard members of the crowd announce our presence.

"It's da 5-0!"

Ignoring the comments, I asked one person in the crowd what had happened and if anyone had been hit.

"Father Panik Village, the most notorious housing project in a notorious city."
- The Los Angeles Times

"Some crazy motherfucker's shootin' his gun out dat window!"

"Then what's everybody doing standing out here where they could get shot?"

"I don't know, ax' them! Shootin ain't nothing 'round here. You know dat!"

My partner tried to disperse the crowd. "Alright, everybody take off before somebody gets hurt!" All the while we had our eyes focused on the third story window. Some people started to leave, but many stayed sensing a show coming.

"Which apartment is it?"

"The one with the gun stickin' out of it!" one smartass in the crowd replied. We saw the shotgun being pointed out of the window for a brief moment and we instinctively used our police vehicle for cover, as did the crowd, expecting shots to be fired again. We were in plain view of the shooter.

"Red 42 on."

"Go 42."

"Red 42. Black male has a shotgun pointed out of the window. Tell 41 to use caution on their approach. We'll be up on the third floor."

"10-4 42, watch yourselves. Did you copy that Red 41?"

"41-Roger that!" Wailing sirens were heard during their radio transmission.

We reached the door that accessed the stairwell to the building and upon entering we had to pass by several young black children who were seeking safety from the gunfire. As we passed them one said, "Look 'it them, look 'it they guns!"

An older youth about thirteen years old told his friend, "'Dey the downtown white police!" They called us the 'downtown white police' in reference to the Downtown Headquarters of the city police, which was comprised of mostly white males at the time. This was in contrast to the Housing Authority, which was exclusively minority.

We paid them no mind as we ran up into the feces and urine soaked staircase littered with hypodermic needles and empty crack vials. After climbing three of these disgusting flights, we reached what we believed to be the suspect's apartment door. My partner took position on one side of the door and I took the other, so that if the suspect fired a shot at the entrance neither of us would be standing in the line of fire. "It's the police! Open the door and make sure that shotgun's not in your hand!" No answer. With our guns still at the ready, my partner asked if we should wait for backup, but both of our instincts told us it would not be wise to wait. Our hand radios on our belts signaled.

"41! 41 on! You're gonna have to get someone else to cover 42! We just got sideswiped-we can't back 'em up!"
In their haste to come to our assistance this radio car was involved in an accident.
"10-4, 41. Are there any injuries?"
"Negative Radio, just get 42 some cover!"

Several east side cars transmitted their requests to assist. We did not wait for cover though, because if we waited any longer the situation could escalate and backup was not coming any time soon. I never liked giving anyone too much time to think when they are about to do something stupid. Sometimes surprise is a good weapon. The door came down with two kicks and we both went in with our guns pointing, expecting to get into a close quarters shootout. The black male was standing in front of the window looking as though he wanted to jump out, but being on the third floor, he thought twice about it. The shotgun was still in his hand and his eyes had a look of desperation. These are those moments when you hear nothing and see in a tunnel only what is in front of you, and your senses are heightened. "Drop that shotgun- don't do anything stupid!" I yelled.

In an instant, today he could live or die; it was his choice. My partner and I faced the same dilemma as he did; should we shoot now? During my career I have encountered many of these occasions where my gun was drawn and an armed suspect could have been shot legally. This is the moment that defines what kind of cop you are. You can take the shot, it would be righteous and you would be the one going home that night, or you could take a chance and allow him to put the gun down and let him live.

"I don't know what to do. I don't wanna move. Please don't kill me."

He wanted to live.

I walked up to him slowly with my gun pointed at his face. "That's right then, don't move." He was frozen in place with the shotgun in his right hand, and I took it from him easily. My partner took him to the ground and handcuffed him without any resistance. All three of us let out a sigh of relief. I can tell you that in a situation like this, one where you are about to shoot someone or get shot, your heart is racing at a rate you rarely encounter. Your adrenaline is coursing, and when you come down from that it is indescribable. Sirens were heard in the distance. During this encounter I did not hear dispatch call us for our status so they ordered a Signal 32, meaning Officer Needs Assistance, because we had not responded. Several police cars were racing towards our location thinking we were in trouble. I called Radio.

"42. Situation under control. Suspect in custody, slow the cars down."
"42! [pause] 10-4. All vehicles headed over to building 26 slow it down... Slow it down."

CHAPTER 2

EIGHTEEN

1978: Youngest police officer in the history of Bridgeport, Connecticut.

I came from a poor family of Northern Italian immigrants and I was the only one of three children born here in the United States. My parents called me "The American" for this reason. I lived and grew up in a section of Bridgeport called the Hollow, a poor multi-racial and multi-cultural area geographically in the center of the city and one that was known for its toughness. I attended Central High School, and after four years of having to deal with racial tensions and race riots, I graduated. I took many undesirable jobs, the very jobs that today they say Americans do not want to do; from digging ditches to driving farm trucks to cleaning floors at the local mall. But I had to work. I needed to start contributing to the household because after all, Mom and Dad could barely make a living with what their jobs paid and I still lived at home. There were not many opportunities for poor white males who did not have the money or the time for a college degree. Wanting something better in life, I thought about joining the Marine Corps.

I always wanted to be in combat and even as a kid I wanted to experience war. The Vietnam War coverage was on television every night and naively I hoped that it would last so I would be old enough to join and go. When we would watch the evening news I used to tell my Dad, who was a World War II veteran, "I'm going to be fighting in that war someday."

"Stupid American! I didn't raise you so you could die in a ditch in this Vietnam!" I was just a kid then, filled with patriotism and the desire for action. The war ended long before I was old enough to join, to the relief of my mother.

At seventeen years old I visited the Marine Recruiter at the Downtown office. After the Sergeant sized me up, he told me to come back after I turned 18. "Put some muscle on, kid." When I did finally turn 18, I had the opportunity to take the test to become a Bridgeport Police Patrolman. I passed the test 18th out of 980 applicants. Sometime later I went back to the Marine Sergeant ten pounds heavier and well muscled. He was glad to see me back and was eager for me to sign up. I told him that I still wanted to join the Marines, but that I had recently passed the Bridgeport police test. In 1978 eighteen year olds were allowed to take the test and become officers if they scored high enough. This was allowed for a brief time, and I actually became the youngest Bridgeport police officer in the history of the city at that age, and one of the youngest in the United States.

"You passed the police test? You're going to be a cop?" The Marine Recruiter seemed surprised. He was the ideal of what a Marine Sergeant should look like; tall, strong, lean, and impeccably uniformed.

"Yes Sir. I'm headed to the Academy soon, but I'm not sure if I want to be a cop over becoming a Marine." The recruiter looked pleased that I was asking his advice, and after looking me over and noticing my worn out clothing and old sneakers, he put his hand on my shoulder.

"Son, you have a great opportunity in front of you and I'm sure you don't have many. Try it for six months. If it's not for you, trust me, the Marines will still be here and we'll be glad to make you one of us. Take the cop job." I took his advice, but I always look back on that conversation and realize what a decent man he was and how few people in my life cared to give me good advice back then.

In the 70's, Bridgeport, the largest city in the state of Connecticut and geographically in the New York City Metropolitan area, was a dying town from what it used to be. This is the same story as many Northeastern cities that had once thrived on industry. It had a reputation as being very dangerous and crime rates were hitting record highs and surpassing the major cities with statistically higher rates of crime per capita; four times higher than the national average, with a murder rate hovering at number one in the nation and always in the top five. Back in its day, the city was a beautiful place with many good, hard working people because there were many industrial based jobs available. When the factories closed down, the jobs went with them and the city began its decay and experienced a 25% poverty rate.

During my career as a police officer, Bridgeport had many housing projects placed all over the city, which at this time housed much of the minority communities. Crime was rampant and the neighborhoods surrounding these projects became battlefields. The police were the only barrier between the good, law abiding citizens living there and the criminal element. There was no one else to take up their cause and no one else willing to come out and protect them. This is why I became a cop.

CHAPTER 3

BUILT FOR WAR

"*S i vis pacem para bellum.*" If it is peace you seek, prepare for war. If anything, criminals have a keen awareness for weakness and strength, timidity and fearlessness. Just as in the laws of the jungle, a predator will attack the weak and afraid. It is the same with criminals and cops. These predators can sense if a cop is capable of handling himself; they can see it, smell it, and sometimes feel it. The uniforms protect us very little if at all. If a criminal is desperate, intoxicated or high enough they will do anything they can to avoid being apprehended. Law enforcement officers today are fatter and more out of shape than ever before. As of 2014, an FBI statistic states that an absurd 80% of cops are considered overweight.[vi] However, regardless of how cops present themselves in uniform, they are tested on a daily basis. Resistance of all types from shooting to stabbing, punching, gang attacks etc, are all things that can be expected on every arrest and encounter even though this is relatively rare.

I would never hit the streets as a cop without the confidence of physical strength. Very few officers workout with weights, train in some form of martial arts or boxing, or run or jog to stay in shape and build endurance for the one time, or many times, they may need it to save their lives or the life of a brother police officer. You cannot shoot everyone that resists; that is a last resort. You cannot stun everyone or pepper spray them. I never even carried mace or pepper spray and we did not have tasers. A police officer that is in shape will be tested less than someone who is weak and out of shape. It is a dangerous job and there is no way around it. Time spent in some type of physical training is an investment for your life and may even prevent you from overreacting when it comes to using physical force.

For instance, in patrol division our shifts rotated but I would always get my five workouts in a week. Even if it was right after the midnight shift I would work out, lift weights, hit the bag and then go to sleep. There are no excuses. Mentally you need to be tough and fit for policing. When you are physically fit and confident in your job, mental readiness naturally follows. Many times it comes down to hand to hand, and sometimes you will not have help at your back. You need to win those battles, and your physical training will kick in. The ancient Roman Legionnaires would say, "Train like you are in battle, and fight your battles like you train." There is also instinct involved, and you can be in good shape and think you are mentally tough but without developing your instincts, you have a handicap. The "do nothings," fearful or lazy cops can only hide for so long. Eventually, if they are on the job long enough, they will face a situation they are incapable of handling. You cannot fake it- thugs will see it. Basically what it all comes down to is this: you have to be built for war.

Built for War

CHAPTER 4

UNDER THE STREET LIGHTS

It is common today to see YouTube videos of police engaged with a suspect and using physical force. The public always views this as police brutality, and sometimes it is, but more often than not it is a reaction the police officer in that position feels he has to make. Unless you are in that officer's shoes, do not rush to judgment. I will not condemn any officer because of a video some jerk posts on YouTube. It all looks bad when filmed. There are courts and judges and a legal system to handle any breach of the law whether committed by a criminal or a cop. We should let the system handle these situations and not our emotions.

✳ ✳ ✳

"Red 42's on."

"Go ahead 42."

"42. Investigating a suspicious vehicle. Two males inside, Connecticut registration XXX-XXXX, on the 400 block of East Main Street."

"10-4 42. I'll run the plate for you. What's the make?"

"42. Uh… Black Chevy Impala. Two door."

"10-4, 42. Zero-three hundred hours."

While on patrol on the east side on East Main Street I encountered two suspicious males in a vehicle at approximately 3:00 am. My instincts told me they were definitely up to no good. I was in a two man vehicle, but working solo that night. The city was experiencing a severe manpower shortage and we were 150 officers below full strength in the department. These were two man cars for a reason. I could have driven by these men because they were not breaking the law at the time, but if you do not investigate something when you have a hunch about it, then you should take the badge off and go deliver mail or serve coffee somewhere and not waste taxpayer dollars. I pulled my patrol car behind them.

What were these guys doing at three in the morning in this high crime area? The decent people who still lived here deserved a cop that would get out of his car and find out. I approached the driver's side, a little behind the door as protocol dictates, and asked him to roll his window down. He looked at me surprised, and then looked over to the other side of his vehicle searching for the second officer that would normally be there if they had assigned one to me on my partner's day off. The two men then looked at each other, and the driver reached for a pistol I had just noticed on his front seat next to the passenger. I did not draw my gun and I do not know why. Instead I opened his door, pulled him out, and threw him into the street. He was big but I was filled with adrenaline. His gun was still on the seat and the other man was eyeing it with eyes wide open.

I told him, "Don't you fucking go near that gun." He didn't. He opened his door and ran as I was ready to draw. The big guy in the street prevented me from getting my gun out by jumping me from behind. I saw him in my peripheral vision and wrestled him to the ground. This happens within seconds, and sometimes there is no time to even think straight. It is three a.m., and most normal people are sleeping.

This was a real street brawl. There was grabbing, punching, and kicking by the both of us and it was not pretty. He made a grab for my tie and tried to choke me with it but it came off in his hand. Cops wear clip on ties for this very reason. He also made attempts to reach my gun, which I carried on a cross draw at this time in my career. Some gun experts will tell you that it is stupid to carry it this way, but I think otherwise. Fuck the experts. Some "experts" have shot themselves accidentally while training others on how to use a gun.

I knew this man would not stop. Throughout our fight he managed to get his hand on the stay in an attempt to grab my gun, which was already undone when I tried to pull it from the holster, but that was the closest he came because I knocked his hand away. At this point, I had to resort to my pugilistic prowess and battered him as much as I could. To my astonishment, it did not do what I intended. 'Shit,' I thought, 'he must be on something.' When you are in a street fight like this you can run out of stamina fast, and if you do and your opponent has more left in him, you're dead. After I pummeled him again, he broke away and made a dash towards his vehicle and the gun that was still on the seat. I followed him and caught up to him just as he was about to reach it. I pulled him away from it, threw him back into the street, and went in for another round. There was no giving up in him and I was tiring.

You never know who you have and what they are fighting so hard to avoid. There was no help, no cavalry coming, no crowd, and no bystanders; it was just me and him in a primitive fight under the lights of a lonely East Side street. One of my punches finally found its mark and he was on the ground in an instant. This was enough time for me to get him cuffed. It was a relief, because I did not have much left in me to keep going. I was in the middle of the street on top of the suspect, just getting the cuffs on him, when two patrol cars came screeching to a halt in front of me.

"Jim! You alright? What the fuck is goin' on here? Who is this asshole you got cuffed?"

In the seconds that had transpired while I had been fighting for my life, Radio had tried to contact me.

"42! …. Red 42 respond….Red 42… do you copy? There are warrants for the owner of that vehicle for armed robbery and Assault One. Do you copy 42?"

"Any vehicles in the area render assistance for Red 42 on a motor vehicle stop with warrants; 42 is not responding."

"31, we're already en route."

"40, we are almost on scene."

* * *

"Red 40's on!"

"Go 40."

"40. Patrolman Lancia has the suspect in custody. He states one suspect has fled the scene, a PR male wearing dark pants and a white t-shirt. Last seen headed towards Nichols Street."

"Is the suspect armed, 40?"

"40…unknown."

Under the street lights. This is where it happened.

CHAPTER 5

DE OPPRESSO LIBER

To liberate the oppressed. De Oppresso Liber is Latin, the ancient language of my ancestors who have been traced back to the Legions of Rome. This is now the U.S. Special Forces motto. However, this motto can also be used for the Alpha Cop who frees the oppressed here on American soil from vicious, murdering criminals who roam the streets, night and day. If it were not for cops who are willing to risk all and stop them, no one would be safe in this, our own country.

There are more people killed on the streets of America than in any war we are fighting anywhere for "our freedom." There is a war on the streets here, whether you want to believe it or not. War is in our own backyard and the people we are protecting are our own families, friends, and neighbors as well as the law abiding good people who depend on us as their first line of defense. And don't forget, the enemy can live next door.

When children are not safe to walk the streets, when the elderly and other innocents are attacked, assaulted, raped, robbed, and killed on a daily basis across the country, I consider them oppressed because they are victimized and terrorized by violent criminals. If you have not been the victim of violent crime, you may not see it this way, but I urge you to ask a victim who has narrowly survived their ordeal or to ask anyone who has lost their loved ones at the hands of violence and criminality. When home invasions, carjacking, homicides, assaults, and all things crime related are rampant and can happen at any time when you least expect it, the law abiding public is oppressed and terrorized. There is a trend of accelerated racially motivated and terrorizing black mob violence sweeping the country and is introducing a new form of terror; victimizing white people for the color of their skin. The fallout of police-thug encounters; the rioting, protesting, burning and looting, is all a part of this war, which greatly affects the very quality of life for Americans. Should we not have the best of the best patrolling our streets and keeping our loved ones safe and our communities from being terrorized? Most people do not realize the full extent of the danger because the media suppresses and trivializes the vital information we need to know for our own protection, while glorifying the very people that are oppressing us.

The answer is not a militarized or federalized police force. All the equipment made for warfare will protect no one but the cop himself, and if he abuses his authority, he will be investigated by the very agency he works for, and the public will have no legal satisfaction or recourse for lack of accountability, and if police are federalized, there will be no higher authority to appeal to for those abuses. So simply put: if the public wants to see what a truly corrupt police force can be, then federalize it. American police forces would look more like the state-run police departments in Europe if they were to become an agent of the federal government. We see the true side of this with the mass immigration/invasion of Europe. Police departments across the continent are turning on their own native peoples when they are protesting this abomination of an immigration policy that is destroying their individual countries and respective nationalism. Using force to disrupt legitimate protests while allowing crimes to be committed by Muslim and North African immigrants, are becoming common practices. Stand down orders given by government officials are also directed to European police when it comes to enforcing the law when it involves a non-European "migrant." This practice, as well as the media cover-ups of migrant crimes, only embolden crime and criminality, and is what we, as Americans, can expect under a federalized police force. When this happens, cops will no longer be citizens in uniforms; they will be government enforcers.

The actual federalization of police in American cities is already beginning. Six cities chosen for a pilot federalized police program include Fort Worth, TX; Gary IN; Stockton, CA; Birmingham, AL; Minneapolis, MN; and Pittsburg, PA. Eric Holder's reasoning for this program was the Michael Brown incident in Ferguson.[vii] Our entire way of life has to change because some stupid thug engaged a police officer violently after committing a crime of violence?

Look at the abuses of the law and the abuses of the Constitution being committed by all federal agencies on a daily basis and ask yourself, will a federalized police force behave any better? Because a cop needs to be ready for combat does not mean he takes on a wartime mentality even though he views violent criminals as the enemy. As a good cop, one needs to be able to turn it on and off when necessary; recognizing the difference between thug and citizen. Being a cop and dealing with violent criminals will never have a uniformed, perfect, Pollyanna outcome. Dealing with violent people has to be met with force when they resist. Plain and simple. It is why the job is so stressful, and the life expectancy of a police officer is significantly shorter than the average person.

De Oppresso Liber

CHAPTER 6

"HERE COMES THE CAVALRY"

"Amber 23."

"23's on. Highland Avenue."

"23 -1500 block of Harral Avenue, third floor, Apartment three-B, neighbor reports a loud domestic. Man assaulting a woman. Caller states the woman is pregnant."

"23. Responding."

"10-4, 23."

* * *

"23's on scene."

Climbing the stairs to the third floor of the brick tenement building in the Hollow, we could hear sounds of things breaking and a woman crying. We followed the sounds to the apartment door where the disturbance was occurring and we announced our presence.

"Police! Open the door!"

We heard a man's voice on the other side of the apartment door. "*Puta!* You fucking *whore*, who called the *cops*?"

I tried the door handle and because it was locked, I looked at my partner and just over his shoulder I could see an old Hispanic woman leaning out of her apartment door in the hallway. She was looking at us with concern, probably for the young woman. She must have been the one who called the police. I nodded at her and then crashed my size 12 boot into the door, knocking it open. I saw a very pregnant young woman in a flowered dress on the floor in the middle of a room that was strewn with broken dishes and spilled food. Her pretty face was disheveled and swollen with welts and she was crying. The male standing over her held his belt in his hand, with which he had been beating her prior to our arrival. He was a medium sized Hispanic and looked like one of the local gang members I had seen before. His arms and hands were bloodied and slashed.

"Motherfucking cops you come in my house like that? This bitch cut me, arrest this fucking whore!" The woman had defended herself during her boyfriend's attack, which I later found out was due to his accusation of her supposed infidelity, and he had beaten her with his belt in a jealous rage. In defense she had picked up a steak knife in an attempt to fend him off. What else could a pregnant 20 year old woman do?

"Hold on, now. Put the belt down." I said to him. Turning to the female on the floor I asked her in a gentler voice, "Ma'am, are you alright?"

"So you fuckin' him too, eh?" The man was enraged.

"Shut the fuck up!" My partner yelled at him.

"Fuck you man! I'm the one who's cut here, arrest the bitch." He turned to the woman, "Like I said, I'm pressin' charges, *Puta*!"

I told him, "Put the belt down, you're under arrest." The woman, who was still on the floor, backed away knowing something bad was about to happen. In an instant, the male ran past us through our attempts to grab and subdue him, made it out the door, and headed down the stairs with the two of us in hot pursuit. I caught up to him on the second floor landing, tackled him, and we both went rolling down the stairs now engaged in a hand to hand fight. The struggle continued to the front entrance of the building and out onto the sidewalk, where a crowd had already gathered due to the noise and the police car parked out in front, and more onlookers were coming. It was summertime and sweltering hot.

The suspect was a member of a gang and was also a drug dealer who was feared by the neighborhood, but of course, they would back him over the cops. "Look what the cops did to Junior, man!" One of the men in the crowd said to incite the others. "They cut him, bro! The cops *cut* him!" Now the crowd, which seemed to total about 25 people, encircled me and the suspect who I was still trying to get under control. His arms were slick with blood from where his girlfriend had cut him, and my hands were also slippery with his blood which made handcuffing him impossible at this point because he was resisting furiously; emboldened by the crowd's support. My partner was at the entrance now trying to keep control of the growing and increasingly hostile crowd as it was encroaching closer and closer.

"Back up, back up! Cuff that motherfucker, Jim- we gotta get out of here!"

"I'm tryin' he's too bloody!" I had him on the ground now but I still couldn't get a grip. The crowd was pressing upon us and seeing the blood and my physical efforts to handcuff my prisoner, they became enraged.

"Kill them fucking cops! Look at Junior! Fucking cops- look what they did!" My partner attempted to silence the loudmouth, but the instigator slithered away while ten other black and Hispanic males in the crowd filled the gap between them. Now came the bottles and rocks. I was just starting to get control of the suspect, and was finally able to get him cuffed. My partner was nowhere to be seen. With all this going on I was now worried about him because he was nowhere in my line of vision. I stood up with the prisoner finally secured when a bottle came crashing down on his head, but bounced off without breaking. I am sure the missile was intended for me. I heard thuds coming from our police cruiser where bricks were bouncing off of it.

"23- Signal 32! Signal 32!"
"What's your location 23?"
"Harral Avenue!"
"All available vehicles proceed to 1500 block of Harral Avenue. Officers need assistance."

At least ten patrol cars responded, advising Radio they were en route. Every cop wants to respond to these calls and to be there when an officer needs help. I have responded to many of these calls myself, and all you can think of is getting there in time and helping your brother officer. These are not called frequently but only when absolutely necessary.

"I called a Signal 32 Jim!" My partner, I noticed now, was at the driver's side of our car with the police radio mike in his hand. That's why they were throwing bricks at the cruiser. I saw him dodge one that came close to his head. "Cocksuckers! Stop that shit!"

The crowd was at a fever pitch now and tried to wrestle my prisoner away from me. This has been done before, not to me, but crowds on occasion have overwhelmed police in Bridgeport and in other cities and have freed their prisoners. I was not going to let them take this guy. They yanked and pulled, then I felt something heavy hit my back- a brick. *"Patos! Maricone!* You don't belong here, cop!" I grew up in this neighborhood, went to school here, and at this point in my life I still lived five blocks from this very location.

"Don't let the pigs take Junior, don't let 'em take him!" The instigator had returned while another brick just missed my face. They were closing in and I knew this was already out of hand. I was making my way towards the car, but the wall of people on all sides of me was making it impossible. At times like these you cannot under any circumstances show fear; if you do, you will be annihilated. I kept telling them to "Back the fuck up" and was making progress, but it was slow progress. I was completely surrounded and all I could see at that point was up, and every window in my field of vision was filled with onlookers calmly watching the show. The wailing sirens heard in the distance began to crescendo, creating an unusual sound. Ten police cars converging towards the same area will do that.

At the ominous sound, the crowd silenced themselves for a moment. They knew that within a few seconds there would be many police cars on scene, and that the cops would be in no mood to play games. The sounds of the sirens became louder and closer, then the strobe lights were visible, and then the green and white patrol cars appeared at every intersection. I cannot tell you what a good feeling that is; it has to be experienced to be understood. The crowd melted away, some ran and some lurked in doorways. Police cars were now on scene and cops were exiting their vehicles in a wave of blue. I was finally able to get to the patrol car with my prisoner. My partner looked over at me with a relieved smile and said, "Here comes the Cavalry."

CHAPTER 7

THE TRUTH HURTS: THE MEDIA

With government propaganda and government staged hoaxes now legalized, freedom of the press is something of the past. News delivered via mainstream media is now controlled and or censored by our government[viii] and includes social parameters which are guided by political correctness. Either way, the public will never receive all the facts to make a rational judgment on current events in this country. As far as mainstream journalism, however, I am only addressing the subjects regarding crime and race and how it is reported today. Who knows what other misinformation we are fed by a government that has made propaganda legal and is known to fund, support, and censor much of what the public hears. We hear what they choose to tell us and only what they want us to know and believe, plain and simple. Has any news agency locally or nationally ever reported factually the truths regarding crime, race, and social issues without skirting the necessary details or blowing them out of proportion?

Large news agencies have actually edited 911 calls, videos, and witness testimonies which would, if told accurately and in full detail, paint a much different picture than the one-sided view they try to sensationalize. The George Zimmerman/Trayvon Martin story is a perfect example of this, among countless others. Meanwhile, media blowhards ignore crimes that are overtly racial in nature and give these absolutely no coverage at all, such as the wave of black on white racial mob violence sweeping the nation's cities[ix] and many other atrocities, such as the Jonathon Paul Foster kidnapping, torture, and murder by a black woman named Mona Nelson on Christmas Eve in 2010. Nelson took Jonathon from his home, tied the little boy to a chair, and then tortured him by burning him alive with a blowtorch, beyond recognition.[x] This vile, racist murder was untouched by the media. How is it that Trayvon Martin is a household name when racism had nothing to do with his death, and racially motivated murder cases such as the Foster child along with many, many others go unnoticed and unaddressed? Instead of reporting newsworthy events accurately with facts, the media embarks on witch hunts, waiting to pounce on the rare event of an unarmed black "victim" killed by the police, and then revel in the dissent and upheaval they cause with their biased type of reporting.

For example, two nationally covered instances of interracial rape were the Tawana Brawley incident[xi] and the Duke Lacrosse case.[xii] In reality, the instances of close to 40,000 white women raped by black males annually go unaddressed by the media, and many of these victims are also murdered after being raped. Do you see the hypocrisy here? The Tawana Brawley story and the Duke case are two rare instances of alleged white on black rape, were nationally covered in the news, and overhyped by the media to incite the public. Later the allegations were proven to be false, and the "victims," who were black, were lying in both cases. Kudos to 60 Minutes for true journalism and for actually investigating the Duke Lacrosse case, which helped to exonerate the accused.[xiii]

If it were not for journalist writers such as Colin Flaherty, the people of America would be virtually blind to this racial epidemic unless they became victims of it. His important books *White Girl Bleed A lot* and *Don't Make the Black Kids Angry* are pioneering the way for others to speak candidly about racial violence in this country and are revealing the truth of this very serious issue that is wreaking havoc in our society and further dividing it racially.

Rosa Parks is celebrated for her defiance of a law which prohibited blacks from sitting in a certain area of public transportation. In more recent news and caught on video is a gang attack of black thugs assaulting a white male who was sitting quietly on a train.[xiv] Everyone on the train was black, except for the victim, and no one helped him as he was being pummeled merely because he is white. This to me is much more inciting than Rosa Parks defying a law that relegated her seat to a certain area. She was not assaulted or beaten by a gang of white thugs. Do the media cover the beating of a white man by black thugs on a national level? No. It is not newsworthy enough to them, because the victim was white and does not fit the racial narrative of black victimization, but if the roles were reversed, it would be national news if the victim was black and beaten by a gang of white thugs. Regardless of what color we are, we all need to be able to use public transportation without fear of our race or where we sit.

News agencies take it upon themselves to condone or hide criminal behavior during protests-gone-wild and give just cause or idiotic excuses for criminals posing as activists and demonstrators. At the same time these thugs are portrayed as heroes, the media fails to condemn their destruction of property, theft, assaults on innocent bystanders and business owners, larceny, disrupting normal life and local commerce, and striking fear into the civilian population after the resulting civil unrest. To divert the public's attention from the truth and criminal accountability, the media focuses on alleged police brutality or on other exaggerated social issues, which may or may not be legitimate, but which are never an excuse for mass criminal behavior.

Reporting the news truthfully provides the public with information on important topics that people need to know of and should be told candidly, not veiled in a shroud of political correctness and political agendas, which are meant to indoctrinate or bully us into accepting a politically correct stricture for thought. Mainstream media is the main culprit in our declining confidence in how news is reported and, more importantly, how we perceive each other racially. For instance, the clusterfuck of a news agency MSNBC is hosted by a circle jerk of agenda driven reporters such as Rachel Maddow, Chris Matthews, and their like whose disdain for anyone with a view remotely different from theirs unashamedly reveals their intolerance and prejudice. Another fine example of "prime time" politically correct browbeating is ABC's *The View*. This nest of five cackling sea hags is every man's nightmare. Their non-stop clucking and lecturing of any guest who does not agree with their "view" is typical of mainstream's tactic to silence and bully anyone who wants to speak the truth with facts. Whoopi Goldberg goes into default mode when faced with facts she cannot refute by pulling out her "race card," as if anyone who is not black should not (and cannot) have an opinion on something that directly affects all of us. These shows are typical for mainstream, and are how most important topics are discussed, addressed, and served up to the American public. This is not what news reporting is supposed to be. Period. They spew out their endless droning of propaganda and partisanism and falsely call it "news" or "open discussions."

Shaming and blaming whites, using slavery, past mistreatments of blacks, and pushing the blatant lie of "white privilege" as the catalyst and platform for every social ill is not only irresponsible, provoking, and severely misleading, but it is false and dangerous and many innocent people have been affected by this misuse of the public's trust in the press. In this way, members of the press in the mainstream media function as oppressors of the people, who are comprised of all races and ethnicities. If it were not for alternative news outlets, we would get zero truth, and I believe the brainwashing would be complete.

More recently, the tragic Charleston, South Carolina church shooting, which claimed nine innocent lives, has the mainstream media concentrating more on taking guns away from legal owners and blaming all whites for one demented criminal's actions. Chauncey Devega, writer for *Salon*, claims that all whites need to answer for the Charleston shooting,[xv] which is not only the stupidest, most generalized statement I have ever heard, it is also the most racist judgment ever given media attention with no accountability. Throughout this book I differentiate between thugs and the law abiding citizens of all colors, and even though blacks and minorities disproportionately commit the majority of crimes of violence, I never advocated for blaming any one race as a whole. But these fools get national attention for making jack-ass statements that are anti-white and racist in nature.

The coverage of the South Carolina shootings has saturated the mainstream media along with stories of white racism and oppressed blacks at the hands of whites. This fairy tale has incited more racial division, hatred, and animosity in this country, and has sparked the illogical and racist call to discriminate against whites and disarm them exclusively[xvi] while furthering gun control agendas across the board. However, the mainstream media and our government have ignored the two other mass shootings that have taken place concurrently with South Carolina's. Why? Because the suspects in those cases were black. In Detroit twelve people were shot, one fatally, during a block party.[xvii] In Philadelphia, two mass shootings occurred within days of each other where 17 people were wounded including six children.[xviii] Again, there is no national news coverage, no black lives matters protests, no Presidential statements to the families, no nothing. The public, nationally, is left ignorant and brainwashed.

The government and the media are clearly using racial divisions that are being caused and fomented by both of these entities to eventually disarm the law abiding American public and keep us divided so they can usher in a federalized, militarized police force.

CHAPTER 8

MY FIRST TIME

This type of scenario re-enacts itself almost every day across the nation. These are events that cannot be helped and no blame can be attached except to the person who initiates these actions. As you will see, police react to violence as they are trained with no regard to color, race, or creed. Violent and dangerous behavior will bring the same results to anyone regardless of skin color. Like it or not police officers need to be well trained for the violent aspects of the job. I believe they need to be intelligent, physically fit, and strong. This will actually create less need for the use of physical force in making an arrest. Remember, there are dangerous people on our streets. They are desperate, innately violent and sometimes fueled by alcohol, narcotics, hatred, and rage. A well trained police force needs to be on the streets to keep all of this under control. I think we can all agree on this.

"Attention all South End cars standby! We have reports of a Parks Department police vehicle stolen at gunpoint. Any car in the vicinity of Seaside Park start heading in that direction."

"Blue 13 on the way."

"Blue 12 headed over."

"23's on. Park Avenue, we'll be there shortly."

"All responding vehicles head over to Seaside Park near the P.T. Barnum statue. Meet the park police officer there. He reports being taken out of his vehicle at gunpoint. Suspect is a young white male armed with a handgun. The suspect is in the vehicle… a green and white Parks Department patrol car.

"23's on scene. We have the park cop in view."

"10-4, 23. Use caution, the suspect is armed."

One of my first assignments was in patrol car Amber 23 with one of my first partners, who was another Italian and a veteran police officer. Our sector patrolled the very neighborhood I grew up in and where I still lived; the Hollow of Bridgeport. This is the center of the city and was one of the busiest posts in the department.

It was a summer evening when we responded to this particular call. The park police were not regular police but had arrest powers within the city's parks and had marked cars, uniforms, and guns. They would patrol the parks in the city, and were similar to the park police in New York City.

"Thank God! That guy pulled me out of my fucking car with a gun! I thought he was gonna shoot for sure!"

"Are you alright?"

"Yeah, I'm fine. He surprised me though."

"Where did he go?"

"Right down Soundview Drive" he said pointing, and we could still see the vehicle in question faintly in the fading light. I told him there were other cars on the way and to wait there for them. We could have asked him to come with us, but my partner felt he was too shaken up. We hopped back into our car and sped over to the stolen police vehicle with our lights off. It was dusk and we wanted to camouflage our approach as much as possible.

"23's on. The park officer is waiting at the Barnum statue, unharmed. Have a unit pick him up. The vehicle in question has been sighted. It is confirmed that the suspect is armed. We are making our approach now on Soundview Drive."
"10-4, 23. Do you want to wait for backup?"
"Negative Radio, no time. Vehicle is on the move."
"23. Understood. Use caution."

The stolen police car was moving slowly in the middle of the road, and as we approached he spotted us and took off at a high speed. We were now in a police pursuit chasing another police car.

"23, In pursuit of the suspect vehicle. Headed down Soundview Drive towards Barnum Dyke."

Now we turned our lights and sirens on, warning innocent bystanders to stay out of harm's way during our pursuit.

"All vehicles, 23 has the suspect vehicle in sight and is in pursuit on Soundview Drive headed towards Barnum Dyke."

A jumble of radio calls came in acknowledging our pursuit and advising they were going to engage also.

"All vehicles except for Amber 23 stay off the air."

The chase took us down some of the South End neighborhood streets, and the suspect was driving erratically.
"Fuck! He hit that car! He's still going!" My partner was right behind the vehicle and kept just far enough back so that if the vehicle he was chasing collided with something, he would have time to stop or avoid it. This was not his first police chase.
"Don't do it-don't do it" I said instinctively as we turned a corner and saw a woman about to cross the street. Thankfully she saw and heard the lights and sirens and stopped just in time to miss being hit by the suspect's speeding car.
"We gotta end this soon, man; he's gonna kill somebody!"

"23, we are now on Iranistan Avenue headed towards Atlantic Street." I told Radio over our wailing sirens.
"23, 10-4- keep us informed as to your locations."
"23, now taking a right onto Atlantic Street."

We had made a full circle and came back to where we had initiated the chase. We pursued the suspect back to the park, which is a public beach area on Long Island Sound. We were close enough to the vehicle and tried to ram it, but he turned into an open field, and then jumped out of the vehicle while the car was still in motion, driverless.
"Did he just jump out?" My partner asked.
"I think so, yeah- there he is, across the street!"

The suspect had now started firing his weapon at us and we could see the flashes from it and could hear the sounds they made. POP POP POP.

"He's fucking shooting at us!" My partner said as he stopped the car. We exited, took cover behind the open car doors just like we were trained to do, and prepared to return fire. POP. POP POP POP. His automatic weapon fired again and he was only 30 feet away from us at this point. I could hear several bullets whiz by us. They make a weird sound when they come close. All of this occurred in seconds.

The shooter maniacally screamed something unintelligible between the shots he fired at us.

BANG! My partner's single shot hit the mark before any of mine could. It was still light enough to see what a .38 caliber, 125 grain semi-jacketed hollow point bullet can do to a human being. His shot hit the suspect in the forehead and the force of it spun his body in the air and he did a complete back flip. It is an image I will never forget.

We cautiously approached the suspect with our guns drawn, and his weapon was actually still in his hand. I stepped on his wrist so that if he was still alive he could not pick it up and use it again. I took the gun and I heard him groan for the last time. My partner cuffed him and called Radio.

"23. Suspect is in custody and down. Shots were fired and returned. Send medic, please."
"23, 10-4. Location?"

My partner, who was looking down at the suspect, did not want to speak anymore so I took the radio from him.

"23. Our location is in ball field number five at the intersection of Soundview and Atlantic. Medic will see the strobe lights."
"23, 10-4. All vehicles, pursuit is terminated. Blue 13, meet 23 at his location. Render assistance. Medic Three, respond to that location, gunshot wounds."
"Medic Three en route."
"Amber 23, a Supervisor is on the way."

As soon as I got off the radio the empty police car, which had been exited by the suspect and was still in motion during the shootout, strangely made a wide circle during the exchange of gunfire and came crashing into our police cruiser. This surprised the both of us because it came from out of nowhere as our focus was on the shooter. Some things are just unexplainable. It was probably 15 seconds that transpired between the suspect jumping out of his car, firing at us, and us returning fire at him. This is how fast it all happens. I was 19 and I had just been in my first firefight.

Later as we gathered information on the shooter we found out his identity. He was a white male who lived in a housing project in the South End. He had recently involved himself in drug use and he was under the influence at the time of our encounter with him. He had taken his father's automatic weapon and then had gotten himself killed for the crazy actions he decided to initiate with it.

He was only 16 years old.

It was a righteous shooting and by the book and he gave us no choice but to return fire. I found out later that his parents, who were decent hard, working people, did not blame the police for our lawful actions. The hardships he was causing them while on these drugs led them to believe something like this would inevitably happen to him, and they had accepted it long before. Sometime after this shooting my partner was called into the Captain's office. I waited outside the door for him and listened.

"So how you doing, S? How was your time off- do anything I wouldn't do?" They had given my partner time off after the shooting to unwind.

"I'm doin' good, Cap. What's up?"

"They're gonna give you a Service Award for the shooting last month. You guys did a good job."

There was a long pause.

"That's the first time in my ten year career I was offered a Service Award for anything. All the good things I've done for this city have never gotten noticed, and now I'm offered a medal for killing a sixteen year old kid? Don't bother. Tell them I don't want it. I'm going to have to turn this one down, Cap."

CHAPTER 9

THE "P" WORD

Profiling. This is the politically correct term, incorrectly used, for what cops call observation. We will use the word observation because that is what it is, not the term that everyone has been indoctrinated with. A cop should never be stupid enough to admit to "profiling." Police observe. Criminals profile. Criminals look for the weak, the easy target, the unarmed, signs of wealth- you get the picture. This is not what police do. Do you really expect cops to patrol an area and not observe the people and certain behaviors in their environment?

If a cop does not observe the people in his surroundings, then he is not doing his job properly. Maybe this is what the politicians want. In my department, we were never told what to say to the media, how to write our reports, or to be sensitive in how you mention the race of suspects or victims. Remember, the race of a perpetrator or victim is just as important to report as the gender and the particular crime committed. You cannot leave this valuable information out. If any of my superiors ever came to me and told me how to write a report using race-sensitive parameters, I would have told them to shove it. Nowadays, policing seems to be influenced and sometimes even cajoled into reporting serious events and crimes in a way that fits the political flavor of the day. For example, high ranking law enforcement officials have actually made excuses for criminal behavior by suggesting that victims did not know how to act in an urban environment. Buffalo University Police Chief Peter Carey, in response to black on white racial violence said that Buffalo is an "urban environment" and that students on campus need to understand it is a "different setting."[xix] This is not how to combat crime. How are people supposed to act in front of violent thugs in any setting? Thugs are the ones who are supposed to act properly if they want to move freely in civilized society. We should never forget this fact.

If we did not notice the race of people in our daily police work, more citizens would be the victims of violent crime. For instance, in the high crime neighborhoods I patrolled, when we would see a white face we would have to conclude they were there to buy drugs or that they were lost or in danger. Either way, they were targets. Police officers have saved many lives and prevented many crimes by observing not just race, but behavior. This same irrational public criticism applies to stop and frisk, a highly effective and proven police tactic that reduces crime, but which now is seen as harassment directed at people of color. The use of physical force is another tactic misunderstood and deemed as racist when applied to blacks particularly. When suspects are violently resisting police, the use of force is the only option a police officer has. When lethal force has to be used with an armed and violent suspect, the media and the race bating Black Lives Matter thugs immediately and erroneously call it homicide, such as with the recent event in Chicago where Officer Van Dyke shot and killed the knife-wielding, PCP fueled, menacing thug Laquan McDonald, which wrongly resulted in a first degree murder charge.

There are so many incredible restrictions placed on police officers who are trying to keep the public safe. Here's one for you: at one point it was suggested that in certain sectors of the city, cops were arresting too many blacks and that it was disproportionate. What were they talking about? The neighborhoods we patrolled were 98% minority and these were high crime areas with a disproportionately high amount of police officers to patrol them. The public would complain of seeing too many white cops and said we were racists, that we did not understand the black "culture," and that we were targeting and arresting too many blacks. If crime ran rampant, we were called racists because they said we didn't care by letting it get out of hand. The blame was always pointing to the police instead of to the actual criminal element. To add to this mess, many black police officers complained that it was "racist" to assign them to these high crime minority neighborhoods, and even filed a federal suit via The Guardians, an exclusive black and minority group within the police department, to look into the matter. This resulted in the federal Remedy Order, which protected these cops from patrolling their own neighborhoods by placing restrictions on the amount of black officers in those deployments. Mind you, I volunteered to work these areas, and white officers have always worked these high crime sectors which are hard to avoid in a high crime city. So in most cases, it was the white cop thrown to the wolves, literally, and all the fallout of false claims of racism and "profiling" were unfairly directed towards us exclusively. We were catching shit from everywhere, the public, the criminals, the politicians, and even those who were supposed to have our backs in the department.

From my own experience, it looks to me as if the public is bending over and changing our very way of life for the criminal element. The truth is, it was the blacks that were terrorizing blacks and everybody else unlucky enough to get in their way. Since when do we give credence to thugs and the innocent law abiding people whether black, white, Asian or Hispanic, go unheard and unsupported? This reminds me of a mass case of Stockholm Syndrome, which is defined in the Dictionary as a "psychological phenomenon in which hostages express empathy and sympathy and have positive feelings toward their captors, sometimes to the point of defending and identifying with the captors." Does this sound familiar? If the public, politicians, and upper echelon law enforcement enable and excuse this unlawful behavior, then it will be past the point of ever being able to contain it again. Eventually, criminal behavior will be rationalized to the point of normal acceptance. If anybody can give you an expert opinion on this, it would be me.

FBI statistics in 2014 showed that Blacks comprise 13% of the American population. This small population commits over 50% of documented murders, while many murders and serious assaults have no race documented and many more violent crimes are unreported, so there are many more to be considered here for this small percentage of the population. Ninety percent (90%) of black murder victims are killed by other blacks and every aspect of violent crime is statistically shown to be committed by a disproportionate number of blacks. These statistics were shown in the August 2014 issue of *Time*.

When did we come to the point where we would confuse violent criminal behavior with "white on black oppression" and racism? What do we need to do to make their situation better? Billions in tax dollars have been lavished to no avail. In fact, race relations are way worse than they ever were. People in power are severely brainwashed, cowardly, or dare I say it- there is an agenda of some sort? You tell me when we hear news about the DOJ only prosecuting the rare white on black hate crimes and nothing for the astronomical amount of black on white racial violence.[xx] That is "profiling" by the DOJ, all under the watch of a black President and a black Attorney General who are well aware that blacks commit the majority percentage of all hate crimes, according to FBI statistics. The end result will be that law abiding people of all races in predominantly minority neighborhoods will still be unsafe and terrorized. Citizens in safer, outlying neighborhoods will continue to be the victims of crime, especially with flash mobs and Knockout Games and home invasions targeting whites; crimes that are all racist in nature. The worst result will be that jaded cops will become less vigilant in doing their jobs and will simply look the other way so as not to risk an encounter that would lead to claims of racism, police brutality, and "profiling."

Thugs know how to push cops' buttons and are now less afraid to confront them violently. Police are the public's last defense to prevent brutal chaos, but the public is polarizing the police while the media reports very little about the violence committed by criminal thugs. Fueled by their disdain for anyone with a badge and authority, both the public and the media jump on any occasion when a police officer needs to use force to defend himself or to effect an arrest. Because of this type of biased, agenda-driven media coverage, the general public is uninformed and ignorant and is placed at extreme risk. These sentiments are voiced in Europe also, where similar occurrences are happening. A UK website named *Violence Against Whites* exposes over there what America now faces. An excerpt reads:

> *"What we see in America we are seeing here in Europe, yet we are not allowed to say so. We have reached a point in our society where the truth cannot be acknowledged if it does not comply with an ideological narrative, despite the fact that the narrative is a lie. It is the silence of the reporters which gives succour [sic] to the lie and imperils its victims, for how many lives could have been saved had they had, at least been warned of the danger?"[xxi]*

The uninformed public is vulnerable to criminality, but instead of realizing this fact, they blindly advocate for law-breakers because of their minority race instead of advocating for victims and condemning the crimes committed against them. The opinions of the public are formed by the blatant misrepresentation of the facts and outright lies generated by the media, who give criminals a venue for their deceptions. Turning Michael Brown into a "victim" of police brutality is a good example of this and is a form of negligence and endangerment. Maybe the mainstream media can tell cops how to do it better. I doubt it though, because they would never be willing to get their hands dirty or get off their fat, judgmental asses to do anything that would actually benefit society.

CHAPTER 10

THE TRUTH HURTS: POLITICAL CORRECTNESS

The speech police. The very idea of political correctness circumvents the First Amendment and is revolting to strong minded, free thinking individuals who are not willing to be governed in any way by stupidity, an agenda, or ridiculous ideology. People who live by this "PC" dictum say we have freedom of speech in the United States; however, if we dare say something that we know to be true but does not fit their parameters of political correctness, we are outcasts and labeled racists, anti-Semitic, homophobic, xenophobic, intolerant, and anything we say is nullified. When this happens, the voice of truth is silenced. The hypocrisy of political correct speech manifests itself constantly. The very fact that the words "white trash" "cracker," "Redneck," "trailer-trash," and "white boy," are accepted and used mainstream and with no fear of offending anyone or repercussions, goes against everything they say is wrong with words such as "nigger," and even using the term "illegal alien" instead of "undocumented." I can tell you that the words so freely used to insult whites are just as offensive as those that offend blacks or Hispanics.

This double standard fits nicely into the hypocrisy and bias of the media. You cannot have harmony between the races if one race can be blamed, punished, and assaulted both verbally and physically, while the other is justified and supported due to an over-hyped and exaggerated oppressed past. I believe the worst violators of "politically correct speech" are the hypocrites who espouse it themselves, and it all begins in certain branches of our own government and progresses through to the schools our children are taught in.

Outspoken and vehement racist, Ayo Kimathi, worked for the Department of Homeland Security and had been placed on paid leave for his racist statements and advocacy for killing whites after many complaints due to his disturbing behavior. His endeavors to incite a race war continued just days later when he publicly said the race war he has been promoting has already begun. He wants to "kill a lot of whites," and engage in an "ethnic cleansing" of what he deems race traitors or, to put it in his words, "black skinned Uncle Tom Koons." [xxii] Basically, black people who do not believe in white genocide are traitors to their race, according to this racist, anti-white murder-advocating imbecile.

Is this the best our Department of Homeland Security can do? Again if roles were reversed and this asshole had been white, it would be national news and he certainly would have been fired without pay. Fellow employees were also quoted as saying that if he had been fired, they were afraid he would go "postal" on them. [xxiii] This is the same DHS who has targets for firearms practice featuring all white "possible suspects" including pregnant women, the elderly, and children. I also would like to know why this man who insists on terrorizing whites is not on the DHS's domestic terrorist list instead of being employed by them and paid with our taxpayer dollars.

Eric Sheppard, a student at Valdosta University, "protested" by stepping on the American flag and wrote a raging letter filled with hate for whites, and submitted it to the local newspaper. In his rant he says, "we kill the white men, we kill the white women, we kill the white children, we kill the white babies, we kill the blind whites, we kill the crippled whites, we kill the crazy whites, we kill the faggots, we kill the lesbians, I say god dammit we kill 'em all," [xxiv] Where is the outrage for these statements by the mainstream media or politicians? This is terrorism and terrorist threats directed at the white population's men, women and children. He should also be on the DHS domestic terrorist list or at least condemned by the media, not given a forum for hate speech on a college campus.

In Cleveland, Texas an 11 year old girl was gang raped by 28 black males for nearly four months. The newspapers and local news stations only described the rapists as "Texans," or "eighteen young men and teenage boys," not 28 black males who gang raped an 11 year old Hispanic girl. There goes your "political correctness" again. The *New York Times* actually did report the incident; however, they blamed the little girl for the assault and quoted community residents who stated, "She dressed older than her age, wearing makeup and fashions more appropriate to a woman in her 20s. She would hang out with teenage boys at a playground."[xxv] Who cares how she was dressed? She's an 11 year old who was gang raped by 28 pieces of shit! These are the people the media tries to defend or cover for? Why would they even do that? Talk about glorifying thugs! It is outrageous how these horrific stories are reported, and I wonder if they would report it the same way if it was a relative or a child of their own. Hypocrites beyond belief! Where are the children's rights advocates or 'violence against women' advocates? These are the thugs that assholes hold up signs for at "black lives matter" rallies and completely ignore their criminality and at the same time, disregard the plight of their victims. Anybody who supports, excuses, or condones the actions of these thugs is complicit in their criminal behaviors.

Quanell X, a leader for the racist hate group, The New Black Panthers,[xxvi] defended the rapists and blamed not only the little girl for the gang rape, but somehow found a way to incorporate white racism into the blame. Moronically, he blames the arrests of the black male rapists on whites.[xxvii] This racist is not alone in this insane mindset of defending thugs from any type of personal responsibility and accountability for criminal behavior, while trying to spin some idiotic race-baiting web of lies. Quanell X even offered support for the black woman, Mona Nelson, who was convicted of kidnapping, torturing, and then killing little Jonathan Paul Foster by burning him alive with a blowtorch.[xxviii] These stories are just a drop in bucket of the daily atrocities that are committed and that promote racial hatred. Suppressing the horrific realities of these atrocities has inexcusably become an accepted part of the political correct society we have allowed to be created. Anyone who espouses political correct ideals and speech is a coward, and does not stand for racial harmony, equality, and personal freedoms.

CHAPTER 11

THE HOLE

Outskirts of the worst housing project in the United States.
Notice the dents on the roof of the vehicle created by thrown bricks.

The P.T. Barnum Apartments, Beardsley Terrace, Greene Homes, Marina Village, Success Village, Trumbull Gardens, Evergreen Apartments, Pequonnock Apartments and Father Panik Village. These were the major housing projects in Bridgeport and they all had their problems with violence and crime, but Father Panik stood out as the worst of the worst. Father Panik Village was the sixth largest public housing project in the United States, the largest in Connecticut, and rated the worst in the nation according to FBI statistics.[xxix] The nastiest area in this particular housing project was an infamous alley called "The Hole." This was, without exaggeration, a warzone within a warzone and we were the only law.[xxx]

Major newspapers across the nation recognized the dire situation in Bridgeport as the worst in the country. In fact *The New York Times* reported that, in an unprecedented move, the City of Bridgeport placed concrete "Jersey" barriers at 40 intersections surrounding the vicinity of Father Panik, in order to deter and stem the tide of the out of control drug trafficking and the related gun violence. [xxxi]

In 1987 an article was published in the *Chicago Tribune* about Bridgeport's housing projects and Father Panik Village in particular:

"One Bridgeport development--Father Panik Village--is as bad as public housing gets, and the other six aren't much better. 'I've been in the South Bronx, Brooklyn and Harlem, and Father Panik is the worst I've seen,' Craig says. "It's too massive. You have 1,100 units spread out over 48 acres.'" [xxxii]

A Salt Lake City news outlet also reported on Father Panik Village and described this portion of the city this way:

"A menacing sight looming on both sides of Interstate 95, the Bridgeport skyline seems to warn visitors to stay on the highway. Dormant smokestacks, boarded-up factories and graffiti-covered buildings reinforce this city's image as Connecticut's embarrassment. The latest blow came June 6, when Bridgeport became the largest city to file for bankruptcy since the Great Depression... Federal officials rank Father Panik Village among the worst housing projects in the country." [xxxiii]

The *Los Angeles Times* described this section of our city as, *"Father Panik Village, the most notorious housing project in a notorious city."* [xxxiv]

The New York Times reported:

"Nearly half of the slayings in 1986 could be traced to two public housing projects here, Father Panik Village and P. T. Barnum, and their vicinities. These overcrowded, dilapidated complexes, a maze of buildings and darkened hallways, serve as virtual incubators for crime... The murder rate here in 1986 exceeded the national average by more than four times. It was the city's highest rate since 1981, when 42 homicides were reported. Indeed, the rate of homicide per capita in Bridgeport exceeded the rate in New York City, records show." [xxxv]

Besides the thousands of residents that called Father Panik home, there were countless fugitives and felons from other cities who would come to do their business and to hide out there, which made it a perfect haven for criminals of all sorts. At one time Father Panik, and especially the Hole, had become so infamous that the city had to put six police officers on walking patrol there, and they placed a new police precinct smack dab in the middle of it. It was a true "Fort Apache" surrounded by hostiles. All the officers from my platoon assigned to this detail were white males because of the Remedy Order enacted by the federal government mandating race-selections for high crime areas. [xxxvi] Normally I would be in Red 42 patrolling this post, but for a time that seemed an eternity, the Mayor put pressure on the department to do something about the hell that was Father Panik. They felt a six man walking patrol, in addition to the two cars assigned to the area which were Red 42 and Red 40, would solve all their problems.

Outside the "Fort Apache" precinct, FPV.

After lineup and before going out on our shifts, our Lieutenant pulled the Red Sector cops aside. "Alright men, I've got something to tell you. I know you're already assigned to the Red Sector in patrol cars but we've gotta make a few changes temporarily. I need to send my best men to work the new precinct in FPV." He paused to scratch his balding head. "You guys are gonna be on a six man walking patrol, and you're gonna walk the Village- old school."

"Foot patrol twirling nightsticks, Lieutenant?"

"That's right, T. You'll be carrying your sticks but twirling's an option."

"Fuck," I said, "How long are we gonna be doing this?"

"Not long, but we can't put rookies in there- they'd get themselves killed, and we can't put women in there because those fuckers will eat them alive. Remedy Order says you guys are the grunts for this. You need to be very visible, no sitting in the precinct."

"Oh, we'll be visible. It's not like they've never seen us out there before." I said.

"You guys are my best. Do the job like you always do it and stay safe. This detail won't last long. Oh, one more thing; the Hole's getting way too wild. Mayor says it's making the city look worse than it already is, so make sure those animals don't get out of control. It makes us all look bad."

Picture a nightmare of concrete, bricks, graffiti and the ugliest buildings you have ever seen. Add to this vision broken windows, litter, empty crack vials and hypodermic needles, burnt out and stripped vehicles, and garbage dumpsters constantly lit on fire. Then picture hundreds of lurking and dangerous thugs, drug dealers, murderers, addicts, thieves, fugitives, and rapists- most of them armed and all of them filled with hate. Then envision the constant threat of snipers, ambush, and bricks thrown from the roofs of many buildings. Pack all these images into a narrow alley, surrounded by the aforementioned structures, with no night lighting and with the ever present smell of urine and dog shit, and you have an idea of what the Hole was like. Just an idea of it.

Everybody on the street here knew who I was, and the other Red Sector cops were not strangers to them either. This was truly the front line of a war during the height of the crack epidemic, and we were the search and destroy mission. Every day brought its usual criminal activity in this place so I will only mention a few things that represent the norm on an everyday basis, because after seeing so much of it, it all blends together into a mash of the same thing. One day in Father Panik would give enough war stories for most cops to tell for the rest of his life. Homicides, shootings, stabbings, drug deals, drug overdoses, heroin and crack addicts walking the streets in a zombie-like state at all hours, domestic disputes, stolen car chases, assaults, and everything else that goes along with the misery of urban policing in the 1980's- it all becomes normal, and it became normal for me. It was a part of my every day patrol. For what was left of the decent people who still lived there, this also became a part of their everyday life. The sad part was, we could not even talk to or interact with them because they would be punished for just being seen with us, so they lived in constant fear, and we patrolled this place feeling that everyone was our enemy.

Walking patrol at the height of the crack epidemic during the highest crime rate in U.S. history.

Several seemingly endless months went by as we pounded the pavement twirling our nightsticks, handled calls, made felony arrests and kept the limited amount of peace that existed there. On one particular shift our Captain decided to join us in our foot patrol so he could directly report to the Mayor what he saw. This was a Captain that was used to being inside and had not been out on the streets like a real cop for years. A desk and a promotion will do that. He chose me and my partner to patrol on foot with throughout Father Panik and into the Hole.

"Alright guys, show me what you do."

"Well this is about it, Cap," I said as I was spinning my nightstick in my hand. "Until something happens- and it will, we just gotta be ready for whatever comes. We walk around and make sure they see us." Right after I said this, automatic gunfire from the other side of the project rang out. POP POP POP POP POP... POP POP POP POP...POP... POP POP. My partner and I were used to this and did not pay it any mind because it sounded far enough away that we knew they were not firing at us. The Captain, however, made a short ducking movement revealing his fear and how long it had been since being a cop on the street.

"FPV Foot Patrol, Unit 3."

"Go ahead." We normally would be more professional on the radio, but we had had enough of this dirty detail, and there was nothing more our superiors could do to us that would have been worse than walking this post.

"Reports of automatic gunfire around building ten. Handle that."
"Yeah, 10-4." Assholes.

Martin Luther King Drive, a.k.a. "The Drive"- FPV

"Alright Cap, you ready to dance?" I asked him smiling.

"We calling for backup?" he asked.

"If I called for backup every time we heard gunfire… ah, forget it. No, Cap, we'll be alright. There's three of us." My Captain did not take any comfort from that. During our walk to investigate the gunfire we took him through the notorious Hole. When you are walking a beat in a project like Father Panik, no matter how much experience you have, there is always that sense of vulnerability because any asshole can make a name for himself by taking a potshot at you and escaping through the maze of buildings. My Captain felt it, and even though he tried to act impressive in his gold Captain's bars, he chose to walk safely between my partner and me in his new found respect for us. It was a typical busy evening and chants of "5-0, 5-0" were heard. They would sound off "5-0" at the approach of cops, whether we were on foot patrol or in a police car, to alert the others of our presence.

"The looks these people are giving us!" My Captain said.

"Captain, everybody here wants to kill us, you have to understand that, and if they had the chance to do it- they would. The uniforms give us very little protection, that's why we do the job the way we do it. We have to take control. Like *this*." I told him, and then approached three particularly menacing looking thugs. The largest of these three had a look on his face as though he wanted to hang us on meat hooks. I wanted to show the Captain how it had to be done here.

"Uh oh, Supercop look pissed! What's the matta, 'dey take yo' police car away?" Someone called down from one of the third story windows in the alley.

I paid the voice no mind as I approached Mr. Meat Hooks and asked him, "Who the fuck are you looking at?"

"I's just lookin'! I kin' look anywhere I want! 'Dis the Hole."

"I don't like being eyeballed with that stupid look on your face- turn your head the other way!" The Captain became very nervous when I said this, but he said nothing. When the thug didn't turn his head quick enough I pointed my finger in his face. "I said turn your fuckin' head!" He turned it away like I told him to, and he kept it turned. This definitely can cause a riot, but I really did not care. I was not going to let these assholes intimidate me and try to make me think that there is a place anywhere in this city that, as a cop, I would avoid and give them a safe haven. Not me. I always backed my actions up, and they all knew it. They had a healthy fear and respect of me. This is why even though they outnumbered and outgunned us over-whelmingly, they chose not to retaliate. Even the most dangerous thugs need to know the cops are still the Alpha dogs.

As we continued our tour of Father Panik, my Captain asked me if I thought my recent actions were wise for keeping the peace. I hesitated for a moment and then told him, "Captain, it's the way I handled that guy in the Hole that keeps this place from being completely out of control. They have to fear me and respect this uniform. These are criminals; they are not oppressed citizens. There's just no other way to do it."

We were the grunts for the most undesirable post in the nation.

About a week later I was called into the Captain's office.

"Lancia, I got a citizen's complaint here and I'm pondering whether or not I should give it to Internal Affairs."

Not in a particularly good mood I said, "Go ahead and give it to those I.A. dickheads, I don't give a shit. What is it about anyway?"

"We have a brutality complaint here stating you grabbed a black male by the neck and flung him bodily into a pile of garbage somewhere in the vicinity of the Hole."

"Oh, you mean the crack dealer that I arrested? The one who ran, resisted, and took a swing at me? He may have ended up in a pile of garbage somehow, but it was a good arrest- lots of confiscated crack as evidence. I can't help that there's fucking trash everywhere- he also stepped in a pile of dog shit while I was chasing him, is he blaming me for that too? Does the Mayor think that just because you put blue uniforms in there everybody's gonna all of a sudden behave themselves?"

"Lancia, you can't talk to me li-"

"Do you want me to do my job or not Cap, because I'm not gonna be a babysitter!"

Part of the FPV walking patrol detail.

Shortly after my visit to the Captain's office I was transferred back into Red 42, same post, only now I was back in my patrol car. I guess we can call it a step up. As I've said before, once you work in the worst, most dangerous post in the United States anything is a step up, but this was exactly where I wanted to be. I was never idle during my walking patrol assignment. My partner and I made many felony arrests and did more than we were ever expected to do. I believe we were transferred because the Captain thought me being on foot would be a volatile mix with the element there. Maybe he was right. That must be the kind of wisdom you get sitting behind a desk. Before our transfer however, one redeeming event happened and it was a rarity.

On a particularly hot summer day our units were on Martin Luther King Drive, the epicenter of the Village, with all six of the walking patrol. We used to congregate at times in front of the precinct located here for a show of force and to see other friendly faces.

"Hey Lance, why the fuck are you still carrying that old wooden nightstick?"

"Because it does the job and doesn't look like I'm carrying a twenty-four inch black plastic dildo like the one you're stroking." We all laughed.

One of the six then said, "They said this was gonna be a short detail. Seems like we've been here forever. What good does it even do? I got six years on this fuckin' job and I get stuck on this shit detail."

"Well you're one of the best I've got, *Son!*" Patrolman G answered, imitating the Lieutenant.

"Then maybe I should be one of the worst and get a cushy detail in the North End like those do nothings."

"You'll have to buy them coffee and kiss their asses," I told him.

"I'll have him bend over right here if it gets me outta this place!" We all laughed again.

As we finished our barrage of complaints and sad-sacking, we all turned to see a young black woman wearing a nurse's uniform walking on the sidewalk towards us. She was pushing a baby in a stroller, which was a rare sight. We watched her approach, wondering what her gripe would be. When she reached us she stopped the carriage and smiled, flashing beautiful white teeth at us.

"I just want to let you know, you officers are doing a fine job. It's good to see you out here and I finally feel safe. I could never walk my baby in her carriage before today. Thank you."

I actually tipped my hat to her and said, "You're the first person who ever thanked us for anything out here. If anybody ever bothers you, let me know." She smiled again and walked away. We were all quiet for a while after that. It was really hot that day.

A typical day on patrol in FPV. Stolen and stripped cars, domestic disputes, drug deals, drug overdoses, burglaries, armed robbery, shots fired, homicides, rape, physical assaults, larceny, arson and everything misery related. We were the ones who came when they called for help.

CHAPTER 12

THE I.A. DICKHEADS

Any real cop hates these guys. Any real cop wouldn't want to work in internal affairs. I am sure you need some type of investigative arm to weed out the bad cops, but these guys rarely did that. The bad cops were still bad, but I.A.'s focus of attention seemed to be on the cops that did their duty because when you do, things get messy sometimes. It rarely goes smoothly. Police officers are human and can make mistakes while making split-second decisions in some of the most trying circumstances. This does not mean they are bad or bad at what they do. In an urban, high crime setting, a real cop gets complaints made against him, even when he does everything right. If you don't get complaints, you're not out there working. The people that made complaints against me, for instance, were usually drug dealers I arrested, suspects resisting arrest for whatever violation, men that preyed on the weak, thugs, drunks, angry mobs, those under the influence of narcotics, or just plain old nasty characters who thought that if they made a complaint it would help their case in court. I accumulated plenty of these during my tour because I did my job well. You can go twenty years and retire and never get a complaint, as many cops do by collecting a paycheck, eating your doughnuts, getting to the calls late, giving up on a foot chase, not getting out of your car to investigate a hunch, or just by turning a blind eye. These are what we called "Do Nothings."

What I especially did not like about the Internal Affairs Investigators was that even though they knew you were an honest working cop, they worked hard to try to burn you when they got the chance. If they worked that hard trying to weed out the bad cops, the department and the public would have been better off. I believe this is the same in any city police department. I can tell you that of all the complaints I did get doing my job, I was never once disciplined, nor did I ever receive any reprimand for any of them. That is because they were all bullshit. For instance, I was called into Internal Affairs on a complaint that was made against me by several "concerned citizens" after a particular arrest I made in Father Panik Village. This particular complaint is representative of the many false complaints made against police officers in the field when they engage in real police work.

"Alright Patrolman Lancia, as you know we have a serious citizen's complaint here regarding an arrest you made recently in FPV. Do you recollect?"

"I make many arrests in Father Panik. Why don't you enlighten me."

"It says here in the complaint that these citizens witnessed you brutally assault a black male running away from you. Do you deny this?"

"Do you have a copy of the report I wrote regarding this incident Detective X?"

"I do."

"Did you *read* that report Detective X?"

"I did. But I'm asking the questions, here."

"I will answer your questions as long as you know the facts."

"Well then you tell me what happened. Because this group of citizens said tha-"

"I don't care what they said. I'm gonna tell you what happened, then *you* investigate it." I picked up a copy of the report I had made, and read out loud what I had written on it.

"'While on patrol in Father Panik Village on Waterview Avenue we observed a black male leading another black male in handcuffs to a parked vehicle. We approached said black males to investigate. Upon our approach, one black male started to run and I chased him on foot. Patrolman P remained and secured the handcuffed male. After a brief foot chase, I caught up with suspect several buildings away near Martin Luther King Drive. Suspect turned and attempted to pull a weapon which I observed as a handgun in a holster on his belt. To prevent him from doing so, I tried to restrain him but suspect attempted to strike me. Using the least amount of force necessary to make this arrest, I punched suspect in the face in order stop his efforts to resist or to do bodily harm to me with his weapon. During this altercation, a large crowd gathered yelling and screaming, "Let him go, you fucking white pig" among other racial threats made towards me as I tried to secure the prisoner. After subduing prisoner and handcuffing him, his gun was confiscated, a .380 caliber pistol, as evidence. I was attempting to escort my prisoner back to the waiting patrol car on Waterview Avenue when this crowd of approximately 20 hindered my efforts. They began to throw bricks and bottles, continued their threats, and being alone with the prisoner and feeling threatened, I had to draw my weapon to be prepared to protect myself and the prisoner in my custody from bodily harm. The threats became even more menacing when I heard someone in the crowd say, "kill that fucking cop, kill Supercop." At this point several police cars arrived on scene to render assistance. Red 41 transported my prisoner to headquarters and I walked back to my partner, Patrolman P on Waterview Avenue. Upon investigation, we found that the handcuffed Subject O was being forcibly taken in handcuffs and was going to be executed by Suspect X, which our intervention prevented. Subject O states they were both drug dealers fighting over territory.'"

When I was done reading the report Detective X smiled.

"It looks like you made a good arrest! I know you're a good cop, but I still have these people here saying you pointed your gun at them and yelled insults back at them. Is that true?"

"Does it say that in the report?"

"No, it doesn't."

"Then it didn't happen."

"They said you called them 'Niggers.' Is that true?"

"Does it say that in the report?"

"No, but-"

"If it's not written in the report, which is a true and accurate account of the arrest, then it did not happen. I did everything the way I should have done it. Who's going to investigate the crowd for throwing bricks and bottles at me and for making death threats against me? Are *you* going to investigate that, *Detective X*?"

"But there is still the problem with say-"

"You know we saved a man's life and took a dangerous drug dealer and a weapon off the streets- you know that, right?"

"Yeah but that's not the issue here. Listen Jim, see the tape recorder that's been recording this interview? I'm gonna shut it off right now." He made an exaggerated show of pushing the 'stop' button on the recorder, shutting it off. He looked at me and smiled. "Cop to cop, what did you say there? I know the people who came in to make the complaint are scumbags and just want to get a cop in trouble. We can take care of that, they're just stupid niggers. Just tell me what you said, I'm on your side."

I laughed and said, "Cop to cop? I don't think so. I said and did nothing wrong. They are lying, and I did my job by the book. We are done here." I got up out of my chair and walked to the door, but before I left I turned to him and said, "By the way, next time you want to talk '*cop to cop*' you may wanna shut that other tape recorder off over there on top of the file cabinet, because the only one who used insulting language here is you."

CHAPTER 13

THE "DO NOTHINGS"

I am not writing this book to make friends or to rally one side or another to any cause. The fact is I have no cause other than the protection of the law abiding and innocent, and the preservation of our Constitution. I speak only the truth of matters and when someone tells the truth, they are attacked by those who deny it and those who are complicit. So go ahead and attack me for it, I am built for that.

Amongst my fellow police officers during my tour on the Bridgeport Police Department, there were many various opinions of me. Some loved me, some liked me, some did not like me, and some even hated me. But they all respected me. There were many that the good cops considered, "do nothings." As I stated earlier they would keep out of trouble, never get complaints against them, turn a blind eye, get to calls late, give up on foot chases, or out of fear let criminals get away with violations of the law. It is easier and less dangerous to do the job this way. The criminals look at them as harmless and, because they keep out of trouble, they stay under the radar. They have no respect, and they know who they are.

The "do nothings" degrade the manpower of a police department severely, because when only ten percent of a police force is actually working, it places a heavy load on the good, working cops. Standards of physical requirements in policing have been completely thrown out the window. Fat cops are the norm, small females, less than intelligent individuals, and those who were never meant to do the job, male or female, have weakened the ranks of modern day law enforcement. These are facts, and many cops today are merely role-playing at being a police officer. They love the uniforms, the perks, carrying a gun, and the power the badge gives them, but they do not earn any of it, nor the respect that comes with these. This may sound callous, politically incorrect or macho, but if you were being attacked by someone intent on killing you, who would you want to come to your rescue? A six foot 200 pound man like the one on the cover of this book with the credentials he packs, or a five foot two female who means well, but will easily be overpowered herself. Or perhaps you would prefer the overweight doughnut eater who couldn't care less about helping you because, unless he is surrounded by many other police officers willing to do the work for him, it would involve too much effort on his part.

Police officers on the job who are physically or mentally unprepared for the rigors of this profession often resort to using their weapons in situations that could be handled by other means, or they allow more damage to be done because they cannot handle the situation at all. They are not built to be cops. That's the truth.

"Red 42."

"42's on- Hallet Street."

"42, meet DB-Five at the corner of Crescent and Seaview."

"42, 10-4."

We were sent by dispatch to meet two detectives to back them up on a case they were working on. We pulled up to their unmarked car, DB-5. "What's goin' on?" I asked them. One of these two men was a good street cop before he became a detective. The other one however, was a jackass before his promotion, and even more of a jackass with his gold badge.

"We need you guys to come with us into the Village. We're looking for someone in particular."

"Alright, what are we getting ourselves into here?"

Detective Jackass looked at me sideways. "All we need is for you guys to be there."

"Well, can you give us an idea about what this is? We may be able to help you out, we know just about everything going on there, we practically live there." My partner asked leaning over me to make eye contact with Jackass. The other detective started to talk but was cut off.

"It's a drug dealer."

"Yeah, what else? There's plenty of drug dealers in the Village."

"I'll let you know on a need to know basis!"

"Oh my God- just lead the way- we'll fucking back you up." I said incredulously. We followed the Detectives into the Village. God forbid they do it on their own without us to protect them. We did not mind doing this, but I did not like his vague explanation of what we were going into. The FBI and DEA were more open and communicative than these particular detectives from our own department on this one occasion. This was not a normal practice by our detectives, but this one was being more of an asshole than he usually was. For the most part, our detective bureau was good at what they did, and actually solved 87% of their homicide cases.[xxxvii] That is as good as or perhaps even better than any department in the country.

Both police vehicles pulled up in front of building 33, and as the usual denizens were milling about, the typical calls of "5-0" echoed.

"We're headed up to an apartment and we want you to take the door down."

"What? You couldn't tell me this before? What the fuck is wrong with you? You didn't even tell me you had a warrant! I guess that wasn't a 'need to know!'"

"That's him! That's him-motherfucker! Get him!" One of the detectives screamed at me while pointing to a running black male who was the subject of his warrant. My partner and I instinctively started the foot chase. We ran together, and while we were running I glanced back to see how closely the detectives were following us. They weren't even running. During the foot chase we came to an alleyway, where my partner took another route to cut off the runner while I remained fifty feet behind the suspect. I was making progress and closing the gap between us, and into the Hole we went.

"Run, DJ, Run! Whitey can't catch you!" At this point I caught up with the suspect and tripped him up by kicking at his legs. He went crashing face first into the pavement. I pounced on the suspect who resisted until I made him kiss the concrete one more time. This calmed him down and I cuffed him and he was searched. He was in possession of a handgun, a .45, and a plastic container filled with vials of crack. My partner, who was breathing heavily, reached us and helped me stand the suspect up. Being blocks away from our police car I keyed my hand radio, but before I spoke into it, I turned to the gawking crowd and told them, "Whitey can't catch him, huh?"

"42's on. We need transport for an arrest in the Hole; FPV."

"DB-Five's on; standby- we're on the way."

"42, did you copy that? DB-Five en route to your location for transport."

"10-4 Radio, tell them to step it up. Large crowd gathering."

The detectives finally pulled up, but stayed at a safe distance just outside the Hole. We actually had to walk through the crowd and over to them with our prisoner. After a few menacing looks by me and my partner, the onlookers were no longer a problem. "Good, you got him. Did you search him?"

"Of course I searched him!"

"Anything on him?

"Yeah, I'm gonna do my report and tag it as evidence."

"Give it to us, we'll do the paperwork. Put him in the back."

We put the cuffed prisoner in the back of their car and I showed the Detective the gun and the container filled with the large amount of crack. "Ah, we got plenty to charge him with intent to sell," the detective said triumphantly.

"Well," I said, "I'm going to write my report and you can write yours. After I tag the evidence, you can do whatever you want with it."

Detective Jackass was not happy, but me and my partner turned our backs on him and made the long walk back to our police car, preferring to walk now rather than sit in the back with the dirt-bag drug dealer.

The next day after this arrest we were called into the detective bureau.

"You guys! Come into my office," Detective Jackass said. "I got a copy of your report here-"

"Yeah, good. What of it?"

"You make it sound like you and your partner did everything!"

"What are you talking about?" I asked him. His face was beet red.

"It was our warrant and should've been our pinch!"

"Okay, so you made the warrant out and you transported the prisoner- I gave you credit for that in my report!"

Detective Jackass actually ripped up a copy of my report in front of me and told me to "Do it over!" Now my blood was pumping.

"Who the fuck do you think you are? That better not be the original -I'm not gonna write it again because the report states exactly what happened. You assholes didn't do anything and you fucking know it! You know better than to do that in front of me!"

"It's only a copy, I was only making a point!"

"We got your guy for you. That's what we did and that's what I reported." I pointed at the ripped report on the floor. "Don't do that shit again! Next time you want two cops to back you up, don't call us."

CHAPTER 14

THE TRUTH HURTS: BLACK MALES

I speak to those responsible for leaving 80% of your children fatherless, without guidance and at the mercy of the influence of thugs. If these are their only role models, they have no chance. For those who choose to wear their pants down to their ankles and manifest any other gangster garbage, nobody is comfortable around you, and nobody will hire you for a decent job. "Pull your pants up. No one wants to see your underwear or the crack of your butt." I am echoing the same sentiments that Philadelphia Mayor Michael Nutter spoke in a speech to the black youth in August of 2011.[xxxviii] You and you alone are keeping yourselves down while destroying the reputation and the positive image of the good, law abiding and hard working members of the black community. Clean it up, and watch the change that occurs. Stop whining and letting others whine and make excuses for you and about your social position- it is in your own hands to change it and not by violence or rioting, but by example and good character. You cannot blame the white man for fatherless households. Thugs cannot blame the white man for choosing a life of crime. Poverty is not an excuse to become a criminal. Many of us, including myself, grew up poor and worked our way out of it. And don't give me any of that white privilege crap-nobody ever gave me anything and I have been overlooked and passed over numerous times because of affirmative action. So stop your whining.

Murders, rapes, robberies, assaults, and drive-by shootings that kill innocent people in black communities are not due to the white man rampaging through your streets. It is due to *you* rampaging through your streets without any care or concern for the consequences of your wantonness. You have become oppressors of your own people and everyone else around you.

CHAPTER 15

THE TRUTH HURTS: THE NEW JIM CROW MYTH

This racist, imbecilic hypothesis and conspiracy theory, believed by some "scholars" and many in the gullible public who are spoon-fed this garbage, asserts that blacks are being suppressed and oppressed by unfair and mass incarceration and kept "down" by a racist society. The fact that I have to explain all that is wrong with this mentality, after all the statistics and realities of crime in America, is astonishing. The fact is, if it were not for leniency and the very real black privilege, as well as overcrowded prisons, many more deserving criminals would be in prison rightfully.

Michele Alexander, the author of *The New Jim Crow: Mass Incarceration in the Age of Colorblindness*, reveals her own ignorance and hypocrisy as she asserts that black males are specifically targeted by law enforcement and the justice system for mass incarceration and the harshest punishments, which render the majority of black households fatherless. So in order for this conspiracy theory to hold water, everyone who serves in the justice system including cops, lawyers, prosecutors, and judges who are comprised of males and females, black, white, Hispanic, and Asian would all have to be racist and complicit in the same "agenda," not to mention the victims and witnesses of their crimes, many of which are black, would also need to be in on the conspiracy in order for this assertion to be true. If anything, it is the poor of all races who receive the harshest punishments, because they cannot afford good legal representation and all suffer from the label of a "felon for life" and all of the lost opportunities that go with it.

Racist, anti-white black judges such as Olu Stevens, Vonda Evans, and Wayne Bennett (to name a few) have openly expressed their biased views in courts of law while flouting equal justice. This is just one of the arguments that fly in the face of the New Jim Crow myth. Couple this with "Bronx Juries," intimidated witnesses, liberal white jurors, and anti-white attorneys and it appears that, if anything, black criminals are being coddled and have been given every chance and excuse not to enter the prison system. This is to the detriment of their victims, their neighbors, and their future targets for criminality. So the New Jim Crow myth glorifies criminals while forgetting the victims of their crimes. In addition, Alexander's arguments only excuse the self imposed plight of certain individuals who exhibit irresponsible behavior in a society with the Rule of Law where we are all accountable. It is interesting to note that a George Soros Foundation funded Alexander's writing of her book. [xxxix]

Walter Williams, an African American economist at George Mason University and author of *The State Against Blacks*, addresses the issue of being black and poor and contrasts the state of blacks from the 1940's and 50's to the state blacks are in today. According to Mr. Williams who lived in a housing project as a child,

"Racial discrimination is not the problem of black people that it used to be. Today I doubt you could find any significant problem that blacks face that is caused by racial discrimination. The 70% illegitimacy rate is a devastating problem, but it doesn't have a damn thing to do with racism. The fact that in some areas black people are huddled in their homes at night, sometimes serving meals on the floor so they don't get hit by a stray bullet—that's not because the Klan is riding through the neighborhood." [xl]

Williams also asserts:

"The welfare state has done to black Americans what slavery couldn't do, what Jim Crow couldn't do, what the harshest racism couldn't do," Mr. Williams says. "And that is to destroy the black family."[xli]

Dying Neighborhoods.
It took less than a generation to destroy this place after integration.

So let us recap here. The actual Jim Crow laws were in effect from the end of Reconstruction (1890) up until 1965. During these years, the statistics of two parent African American homes were astronomically *higher* than they became after the end of the actual Jim Crow laws which were, in fact, discriminatory. So to compare the "state" of blacks today in a "New Jim Crow-racial caste system" (according to Alexander's assertion) to the Jim Crow laws of the past is ignorant and extremely misleading. It is widely accepted that it is the welfare system that has destroyed the family unit of all races, and has relegated recipients of it into a caste system where they are at the bottom. The very premise of welfare for single mothers discourages two parent households, especially if one of them has gainful employment. This welfare system, which could do so much for the truly needy, has been abused and used to create this endemic system of fatherless homes.

Let's use more statistics, because after all statistics are based on facts, not conspiracy theories or myths or even racial biases. Using the popular and widely accepted excuse of 'poverty' to perpetuate the myth of black victimization and racial biases when it comes to crime and sentencing, let's look at the state of West Virginia, the poorest state in the nation. It has a 96% white population, has experienced perpetual and abject poverty, and has the lowest ratio of police officers to civilians. Considering all of this, West Virginia has a low crime rate (about 21% lower than the national average),[xlii] so it is not poverty that causes violence. Now in comparison, look at Washington D.C., even though it is not a state, it has the highest average income in the 48 contiguous states, the highest police to citizen ratio and despite this, it historically has one of the highest crime rates in the nation in all categories, even with the strictest gun control laws.[xliii] By the way, it also has the highest rate of incarceration and an 80% black population. The criminal justice system in D.C. is well represented by African Americans in its police force and judicial system. This means black judges, prosecutors, cops, and victims as well as witnesses are putting black criminals away for committing crimes. Jim Crow has nothing to do with any of this.

We also need to remember that the prison system contains a high proportion of blacks because they commit most of the crime, including white collar crimes, such as forgery, welfare fraud, check fraud, etc. A black male is eight times more likely to commit violent crimes in a relationship. Black males from ages 16-36 make up only 3% of the population, but commit 33% of all crime. A black male is 40 times more likely to commit violence against a white victim than vice-versa. Blacks are also 130 times more likely to rob a white victim than vice-versa. Add this to an average of over 35,000 rapes of white women per year by blacks, including 3,000 gang rapes of white women by blacks per year and you have the reason for the large proportion of blacks in the prison system.

Juvenile statistics regarding crime and race are even more revealing. Black juveniles make up 16% of the youth population, and account for 52% of juvenile violent crimes and arrests, which includes 58% for homicide and 67% for robbery according to the FBI and DOJ stats.[xliv] So, Ms. Alexander, I believe the prison system is doing its job by placing these violent offenders behind bars, but they are also releasing many of them prematurely only to commit violence again.

Alexander also asserts that the War on Drugs is used as a platform for this "undeserved" racism and mass incarceration which causes the loss of fathers and mothers in African American homes. In reality, most drug offenses are strongly associated and proven to be connected to violent crime. The population of drug offenders in federal prisons only accounts for 25% of prison populations as a whole, and they are not all black offenders but include all races. Violent offenders take up more than 50% of prison populations,[xlv] so this element of the author's argument also does not stand on common sense. In my opinion, she makes broad racial claims about the justice system and its "unfair" incarceration of blacks for drug offenses.

Remember, they commit these violent offenses and most of these are connected to drug use and sales. Let's not trivialize drug use. It is still a choice, a bad one. The need for money to purchase drugs leads to high instances of armed robbery, burglary, assault, etc. The sale of drugs perpetuates all of this as well, and adds to the overall statistics of violence; murders, assaults, etc. over territory to sell drugs and obtain them for sale. The use of drugs breaks down the structure of the family, interpersonal relationships, and lowers the quality of life for the user and those they are involved with as well as the neighborhoods they live in. Drug use affects their ability and opportunity for gainful employment, and is a reason for the low high school graduation rate among users. Drug use or sales is not victimless. This is a major problem across the country for all races; it should never be trivialized because I have personally seen the worst of its effects. Most violent crimes and crimes of theft, burglary and larceny are directly linked to drug use and/or sales.[xlvi]

Clearing out a crack house. Notice the mattress on the
floor. Many abandoned buildings were taken over by
crack and heroin addicts. This was dangerous duty.

Here are more statistics that have nothing to do with race or Jim Crow. Drug and alcohol use is responsible for 95% of all college campus crimes. Eighty percent (80%) of all prison inmates abuse drugs or alcohol, and nearly 50% of jail and prison inmates are clinically addicted. Ninety-five percent (95%) of prison inmates return to substance abuse after release from prison.[xlvii] There are repercussions, damages, and human victims of drug use and sales, and it can never be trivialized or used as an excuse for the supposed oppression of a particular race.

I truly believe that if there is a caste system, each individual is responsible for his or her place in it.

How can we attempt to fix a problem that cannot even be discussed truthfully and without racism being used as a stumbling block to gainful remedies? The truth would expose the problem for what it is and would force a logical approach to amending this epidemic scourge. When a felon does his time, regardless of race, they all face the repercussions of having a violent felony on their record. It affects all of them, and is a residual effect of bad decisions, restricting certain rights such as gun ownership, voting rights, gainful employment, etc.

It is also interesting to note that according to the NAACP, there are more whites on death row than blacks[xlviii] even though blacks commit more violent crime not only per capita but the actual majority of it statistically, so even the common public myth of more blacks being sentenced to death is also a farce.

The black community and its "leaders" need to address the epidemic of drug use and the effects it has on their current plight. This is a very real problem for everyone. It is distressing to me that after all these statistics, in addition to the astronomical rates of crime committed by illegal immigrants coming over the Mexican border, that it is the everyday white individual that is blamed for all that is bad. Why do we tolerate this? As long as this idea is allowed to go unchecked it will become a twisted truth.

CHAPTER 16

WTF? 911 FOR COPS?

As I consistently and truthfully discuss throughout this book, I do not agree with everything modern day policing is resorting to in order to "combat crime." The central aspect of this trend is the military mentality of law enforcement that is growing at a dangerous rate. Violent crime was at an all time historic high during my career, and it was much more dangerous to be a cop then than it is now. This comparison is necessary in order to show there is no drastic reason for this new trend. When I was a police officer our department and many other city departments were understaffed and had inferior equipment compared with today's departments. Yet we did not become soldiers or Gestapo units in order to keep things under control. Things were more under control in the past, because crime was more concentrated in certain areas and did not overflow into other neighborhoods to the extent it does today. We did not allow it to.

Telegram/Viorel Florescu

Suspect caught

Bridgeport police escort   , 19, of Shelton Street, Bridgeport, to a police car Wednes-
day. City police chased   through EastSide yards after he ran from federal authorities. He
was caught near William Street. He was sougt on a federal indictment reportedly involving drugs,
police said. Bail was set at $100,000.

One of the many raids I participated in with different federal agencies almost on
a daily basis. No combat gear and we still got the job done.

SWAT: Special **W**eapons **A**nd **T**actics. Today it is very common to see SWAT teams and other specialized units where police officers are dressed in BDUs wearing helmets, body armor, knee pads, and carrying their automatic rifles, all lined up and following each other in a hurried and crouched position. Not only does this all look ridiculous to me, but it is also impractical. I am sure that in some extraordinary situations a specialized unit would be needed, but not as an everyday response team to situations normally handled by regular cops, no matter how dangerous.

While law enforcement officers on scene are waiting for these units to show up and deal with the problem at hand, people die and the damage has already been done or has escalated to a stage that is past the point of a resolution with the least amount of tragedy. Columbine, a prime example, could have been less of a tragedy with fewer lives lost if the police officers on scene had taken quicker actions. Waiting for SWAT for any length of time gave the gunmen the opportunity to kill at will while there were plenty of armed cops who could have stopped it by just going inside. We as police officers are supposed to place ourselves in harm's way for the public. If you are not willing to do it, you cannot call yourself a cop.

I have been in more volatile situations than most of the members in these "special" units will ever see. Cops are safer now than they ever have been, with record lows of cops being killed by gunfire as of 2013 -the lowest in 126 years,[xlix] which is in sharp contrast to past decades when cops were killed much more often. So why all the fear and overkill SWAT equipment? Today SWAT is called out for the emergencies that, when I was active, we had to handle ourselves. Sometimes it was a regular two-man patrol car responding and if you were lucky, you would have backup.

Recent statistics show that SWAT teams are only deployed to situations with guns or barricaded suspects 7% of the time, and more than 80% of SWAT deployments are for search warrants.[l] Since when do we send SWAT to serve search warrants? This is the job of the police and it always has been, but for some reason now we need armored military vehicles and SWAT teams in battle dress wearing ski masks playing at soldier.

Judges are now issuing an estimated 20,000 "No Knock Warrants" annually for "high risk" raids, where police do not even need to identify themselves while they forcibly enter a home.[li] Raids today are no more "high risk" than they were twenty years ago, so this trend is just an excuse to use an overbearing police force without accountability. In some cases many tragic mistakes are made where innocent people are killed, injured, or manhandled and have their civil rights trampled upon. In addition, this new tactic places the police officer in danger because the homeowner, whether guilty or not, is unaware of who is coming in and will instinctively defend his home. This is just bad for everyone across the board which should be common sense, but because it is in practice, we can only assume it is being used for a more nefarious reason or tactic. When officers announce themselves as police, the fear of having your home invaded by dangerous criminals is not a factor any longer. What are judges thinking when issuing these types of warrants? This is irresponsible and places everyone at risk, including the police officers. I am sure a judge who issues a no knock warrant would not want his private home entered, by mistake or otherwise, in the middle of the night with concussion grenades exploding in his child's bedroom. Judges should know better.

One example of many was the botched raid in Atlanta, GA where a 92 year old woman's home was raided by mistake by a narcotics team in possession of a no-knock warrant. Thinking she was being robbed, she defended her home and fired her weapon and missed. She was gunned down by the officers who fired at her 39 times and hit her with five shots. She was killed. When officers realized they had the wrong house, they planted drugs in the home to cover their stupidity and incompetence.[lii]

American SWAT raids are estimated at 80,000 raids per year and counting compared to 2,000 raids in the 1980's,[liii] and crime rates were higher in the 1980's than they are presently. In essence, we have "specialized" cops now handling what regular cops did not too long ago and throughout history. These SWAT units are now relegating cops to the lesser duties of policing and turning them into meter maids and traffic enforcers, while "special" units overreach and handle regular police work with a military approach. The Posse Comitatus Act of 1878 was passed to prevent this very trend from happening, but this law has been flouted, and is now being circumvented by militarizing police units while politicians are pushing for a federalized police force. During extraordinary times, the National Guard would always be available to come out and handle an out of control situation, but these are the only times special units should be called in. I would never have been proud to walk around wearing a ski mask and military equipment policing American streets.

Two strongmen come to aid of police division

By KARLA HUDECEK MORAN
Post staff writer

Two patrol officers — award-winning power lifters — will add some muscle to the Special Services Division by bashing down doors and cruising around housing projects to deter drug trafficking.

The pair, Officers Raymond Sherwood and James S. Lancia, were assigned to Police Supt. Joseph A. Walsh's office last month.

They use battering rams to break down doors during drug raids; transport prisoners from the raids

to the Police Department, and disperse crowds that often gather at the scene of raids.

"They don't do any investigative work," Walsh said. "They're providing uniform drug enforcement.

"They're big, husky, capable and very dedicated police officers."

Usually patrol cars are called off their assigned posts to assist in raids, Walsh said.

With a steady detail at the disposal of the Special Services Division, the post patrols remain undisturbed, he said.

Sherwood and Lancia, who have

won state Police Olympics titles in power lifting in the heavyweight and light heavyweight categories, respectively, also assist officers in emergencies, Walsh said.

Lancia has spent most of his eight years in the department patrolling Father Panik Village and for six months was Sherwood's partner in the East Side housing project.

When the department was at full strength about five years ago, Walsh said, officers patrolled Main Street, Madison Avenue, East Main Street and other heavily traveled streets as Sherwood and Lancia do

now.

In the month that the officers have been working for Walsh, they have made 14 narcotic-related arrests, mostly in the South End near Marina Village, and have assisted Special Services, the Statewide Narcotics Task Force and Drug Enforcement Administration in a number of drug raids.

Sgt. Roger N. Falcone, Special Services commander, said it's important to have one of the uniformed officers operating the battering ram so people inside the apartment or home that's being raided understand that the police are on the other side of the door.

Newspaper article. This was our Chief describing our activity in the newly formed Special Services Uniformed Division. We performed these raids on a daily basis.

CHAPTER 17

WE WERE THE GOOD GUYS

We were approachable and you could talk to us, the typical uniformed cop in blue. Even in the most crime infested areas, the black kids loved being around us and they were the only ones who would not suffer repercussions by the criminal element for doing so. They felt safe around us. They used to grab onto my arms and I would lift them in the air and mimic bicep curls with them- they loved it. Many young black males would approach me and tell me, "I want to be a police officer like you." The only people who felt intimidated by my presence were the bad guys. Cops can be tough on criminals and the law abiding people they are there to protect will love them for it and feel safer.

We were kind and respectful to the people who needed and relied on our help and protection, and hard on the criminals who oppressed them. In today's society cops are criticized by the public for doing their job and how they are trained to do it, and it gets to the point that they are paralyzed and are not allowed to do what needs to be done. The public's anger against cops is fomented by the media and the race baiters of all colors, and the tactics they use to report and discuss certain incidents. The ones who suffer are the people who live in these areas under the rule of the criminal element. So to the public I say this: before your next protest and looting session while taking up the cause of a criminal thug who dies as a result of his own violent actions, you need to think about something. If you hamper police from engaging and arresting the bad guys because of the color of their skin, then criminals will become empowered and unmanageable. It will become so bad that the only way it will be possible to stop it is by using the excuse of Martial Law and militarizing the police permanently; which will still not keep law abiding citizens safe. No one wants this. Even if you hate cops you still call them when you need them. You protest for thugs who would eat you alive on the street if you get in their way or present yourself as an easy target. These are your true enemies. If you do not confront the police in a disrespectful or aggressive manner or lead a life of crime, they will leave you alone. Plain and simple.

Do not place yourself on the same level as a thug, or you will be treated as one.

The public needs to become aware of what is really happening around the country in terms of crime and the racial motivation behind it. Black on white mob attacks, the astronomical murder rates committed predominantly by black males and illegal immigrants, and all the other categories of serious crime are not reported by the media, and if they are, race is not reported unless it is the rare white on black crime. In addition, politicians never address the issues of black on white crime, and it is perpetuating the hatred between the races when cops get tough on criminals, no matter what their color is. These are the elements that create a perfect environment for a major race war: endemic hatred, constant turmoil, and chaos. America and its quality of life are changing for the worse because of this.

Our elected political officials should be held accountable for making our streets a place of fear through their cowardice in addressing the truth and their hypocrisy in hiding it. We should hold the media accountable for having the presumption and audacity to decide what news we hear about. They twist the truth and hide events that, if we were informed of them, we could all be a little safer. The media is a major perpetuator of race hatred in this country.

We were the good guys.

Do the people of America care about race equality and crime when around the same time as outrage for Trayvon Martin swept the nation, two British tourists wandered into a black neighborhood, in the same state of Florida, and were killed merely for being white? Where were the protests for that? Where was the Presidential statement for the families of these young men which was so freely given for Trayvon Martin?[liv] What about the white couple in Tennessee who were brutalized, killed, and mutilated by five blacks?[lv] What about the numerous separate racially motivated attacks on white victims in all the major cities across the nation? Even the elderly and infants are not exempt from their racial hatred and violence and they are also easy targets for these cowardly assaults. There are too many more of these types of crimes to be listed here, which is a shame because they are not even reported by the news nationally.

Violence against women in terms of rape and domestic violence are astronomically higher for black perpetrators on white victims.[lvi] To cover up the astronomical rates of black on white rape, the FBI has, for years, cooked the books by including Hispanics in the category of "whites" as perpetrators for crime stats, but they know the difference between these two races, and categorize Hispanics and whites separately for other federal usages. They even categorize Hispanics and whites separately to show victimization rates. This is a new and misleading statistical tactic that gives a false perception that white on black crime occurs in higher numbers. This is what happens when you have an autocratic law enforcement entity; they can twist the truth, lie to your face, and there is nothing you can do about it.

My point in all of this information is to show that it is not the average beat cop who is misleading you, but the higher ups in law enforcement whether it be city, county, state or especially, federal. These work in conjunction with other deceivers in politics, government, academia, and in the mainstream media to brainwash the common public into accepting their false narrative. In the meantime these same entities have no problem sacrificing good cops, the ones who care about the law abiding and who are the only ones out there working to preserve some semblance of order, to an ever growing hostile public.

In light of this, I ask the question: why *does* the media seem intent on demonizing the good cops who care about the victims of criminal atrocities? It seems that the further distancing of good cops from the law abiding public can lead to the wider acceptance of a "benevolent" federal police department. The sad part is that when good cops speak out against the criminal actions of the very thugs the public, media, and politicians defend, they are quickly silenced, censored, and in some cases, they are fired. This forced censorship creates the notion or the belief that cops are complicit in this agenda. This in turn leaves the public with a politically enslaved police official who has to tow the politically correct line.

There is a simple solution. Let the police do their job as they always have, especially when dealing with violence and violent criminals. We are not your enemy.

The Alpha Cops are still the good guys.

Imagine looking out your window and seeing this. Families still lived here in fear.

CHAPTER 18

HUMAN SHIELDS

As patrolmen and as members of the department's specialized units, my partner and I would be called in from our regular police duties to provide the uniformed arm of a raid, whether from our department or from the FBI, DEA, ATF, or State Police Narcotics Division. If a raid took place while we were working, these agencies would specifically ask for us. They liked our enthusiasm, professionalism, strength and fearlessness. On one occasion we were requested by agents of the DEA to breach the headquarters of a Jamaican drug ring. I enjoyed this aspect of a raid and taking doors down. Most times it was with a battering ram and sometimes with my right foot. Whatever method we used we were always the first to go in. I would like to make it clear that when I did take part in a raid, regardless of which agency it was with, it was done with a lawful warrant and after a full investigation. The raids I participated in were always for major narcotics operations and/or dangerous criminals, and we never involved ourselves in a raid that was for something petty. Today law enforcement uses SWAT units to perform "no knock" drug raids who use concussion grenades for $25 drug deals. This to me is ridiculous for a petty crime, but it is becoming a common occurrence. The Jamaican drug rings at this time were stone cold thugs. They would strong-arm, shoot, and kill their way to controlling the lucrative drug territory in our city. The drugs dealt by these and other dealers of all colors contribute to the moral decay of our already polluted and dumbed-down society.

On this raid we arrived at a three story tenement building on the east end where this particular Jamaican drug ring based themselves, and the building in question was surrounded by DEA agents. No one was wearing combat gear, we were in blue and the DEA wore vinyl blazers with their logo on the back. No grenades were thrown either. With some of the agents beside us, my partner and I took positions on either side of the entrance on the first floor. With the battering ram in my hand and at the signal from the lead agent, I took the door down after first identifying ourselves as law enforcement officers.

"DEA! Federal Agents!" We entered the apartment with our guns drawn and with the agents behind us, shotguns and automatic weapons in hand.

The Jamaican Rastafarians were scattering about, surprised. Some of them were subdued and restrained quickly so they could not destroy evidence. I noticed two Rastafarians headed through a door which looked as though it led to a cellar. My partner and I followed, which is very dangerous because we did not know the layout or who or what was down there. Places such as these are the perfect place for an ambush, especially when the people being chased are dangerous and desperate. It was dark as hell in that basement. I was right behind the two suspects, and I was able to grab one six-foot-five monster of a man by his dreadlocks which forced him to stop abruptly. With a firm hold on his long dreads I put my gun to his right ear and told him, "If you make any move I'll take your head off!" He knew I wasn't playing. After a brief search I found he had no weapon on him.

There were two that ran down into the cellar, so I walked with my suspect with my gun to his head and used him as a human shield. "Your friend needs to come out now!" He did not answer me. Wanting to react quickly, I walked further into the dark cellar, and as I did I could hear the commotion from upstairs. The DEA agents were still busy and distracted, so it was just me and my partner who was right behind me backing me up.

"Fuck this!" I yelled. "I'm gonna start spraying fucking bullets everywhere if you don't come out! I don't care what I hit!" I told the Rastafarian I had by the hair, "Tell your friend to come out and put his gun down, 'cause if he comes out shooting you're gonna be the first to get hit!" Realizing this was a possibility, he immediately called out to his friend.

"Come on out, mon! Dis modafucka's crazy!" The other suspect, who was a clone of the one I had by the hair, took his friend's advice and came out with his hands up.

"Don't shoot mon- I got no gun!" We cuffed our prisoners and my partner found his .45 caliber pistol tucked in the corner of the basement where he had hidden it. Believe me, criminals can sense weakness and if I had not been that aggressive the situation could have been a lot worse.

When you go in first, you become a human shield.
We were made for this job.

My partner and I were the human shields for the agencies that took us with them for their raids. We loved it. Many raids were made with us this way, and I am only mentioning a few that stand out as more than just routine. Routine for me is just kicking the door in, apprehending suspects, gathering evidence, writing a report later and that's about it. To some cops this would be the story of their career, a war story to brag about to women and children, but to me it was nothing and easily forgotten. Sometimes it goes very smooth with no hitches and sometimes not, but every time you do it your adrenaline is up and you never know what is behind the door or how it is going to turn out.

A large inter-agency raid was about to take place with the FEDS, and as usual, they called me and my partner as their uniformed door kickers. We were all assembled in the FBI headquarters of the federal building downtown, planning the raid and being given our individual assignments. This happened to be another large Jamaican drug ring that was being targeted, and while we were discussing it, some agents were sitting at desks, some were pacing, and some were eating doughnuts. The FBI guys had good doughnuts. Not just cops but anybody with a badge and police authority seems to gravitate towards them. I was not a doughnut eater, buy my partner helped himself to one of them. There were a couple of FBI agents with powdered sugar stuck to the corners of their mouths, which was annoying, because they were trying to talk seriously to us about the danger of the upcoming raid.

"So does everyone understand what their job is gonna be? The lead agent asked everyone in the room.

"Yes, Sir," most of the young agents chimed in to acknowledge the instructions. They were excited.

Wanting to lighten up the mood and ease the tension in the room, I spoke up with an exaggerated and ridiculous New York -Italian accent. "So let me get 'dis straight Sir, when we go in- guns blazin,' the guys dat don't get shot are gonna get their asses kicked pretty good. Is tha' right?"

They exploded in a flurry of "No!" "You cannot do that!" "We never said that!" "We must avoid shooting our weapons if at all possible!" My partner was laughing so hard his face turned purple.

"My God, guys, I'm just kidding! You gotta lighten up, we've done this before together- we're all professionals here." As I laughed the lead agent eyed me intently, and realizing I was joking, allowed himself a smirk. When the room finally quieted down my partner looked for the bakery box. "Any more of those doughnuts with the rainbow sprinkles over there?"

The FBI insisted that, for our protection, we had to wear our bullet proof vests. I hated wearing these. It was optional on regular patrol and some guys wore them, but most of us did not. They are very uncomfortable and with my luck it would be my big head that stopped the bullet and not the vest. In those days the vests were white and most of us cops displayed our artistic talents on them. My partner's vest had "Eat Me" written across it, and mine had a skull and crossbones in the center with a bull's-eye over my heart with the words "100 Points" over it. The FEDS were watching as we put our vests on and saw the artwork. A few of them gave us looks that suggested we were not sane enough to go on these raids with them, but they knew our reputation and yes, they wanted us there. Seasoned street cops are very different from Federal Agents.

We arrived on scene and performed the afore-mentioned routine door kicking, me and my partner in first, only this time we surprised them pretty good. Three of the suspects were smoking marijuana sitting on a couch with a white woman. One of them made a motion towards a gun that I noticed was on a coffee table directly in front of them. I was quick enough to reach that gun before he did, but I did not pick it up. I stood there facing him with my gun drawn and said, "Go ahead- pick it up. See what happens." He didn't pick it up.

I confiscated his gun as evidence and the room was secured. Everyone was cuffed and on the ground and being searched- by the book, just like the FBI guys wanted. Now, when you have a warrant for narcotics you can legally tear the place up because the scope of the search, when you are looking for drugs, can be literally anywhere. The FEDS were having a hard time finding the huge stash they expected to be there and knew the suspects had, but it was nowhere to be found. Other than the small amounts of marijuana they were smoking when we came in, there was nothing. The agents were becoming very irritated; these guys do not like to come out of these types of raids empty-handed. One of the Rastas I had cuffed on the ground had actually defecated in his pants out of fear when we entered. It smelled up the room, which added to the overall bad mood.

"I made you shit your pants, huh?" He didn't answer me. The apartment was being torn apart by the agents while my partner and I were watching the prisoners on the floor. After a long and fruitless search, we were getting ready to pack it up when I noticed a Bob Marley poster on the wall. I was in a particularly crappy mood at that point so I turned to the pants shitter on the floor.

"Why do all you pot smoking Jamaicans listen to Bob Marley?" Again no answer. Annoyed at him and his smell, I walked over to the poster and ripped it off the wall. I was going to tell him that he could use it to wipe his ass with, but what was behind it distracted me. An opening in the wall that the poster had hidden from view was now exposed and it was filled with what the FEDS were looking for. The agents were instantly happy as they emptied the wall of its contraband. The raid was now a success and their hard work paid off. Before we all parted ways, one of the agents promised us better doughnuts for our next raid.

Thank you Bob Marley.

CHAPTER 19

THE TRUTH HURTS: FEDERAL GOVERNMENT AGENCIES

Democracy, Republic, Socialism, Communism, Totalitarianism, Dictatorship…America may be a little of all of these, but the actions of our government over many decades and more so today, are the exact definition of Fascism, which in the dictionary is defined as *"a governmental system led by a dictator having complete power, forcibly suppressing opposition and criticism, regimenting all industry, commerce, etc., and emphasizing an aggressive nationalism and often racism."* Either way, it certainly resembles something different from what our Founding Fathers had in mind and what the Constitution was made to protect us against.

Since 9/11 there have been more laws passed to restrict our freedom and privacy in the name of peace, security, and safety than in the past 200 years. The NSA, DHS, CIA, FBI, DOJ, DIA, DOD, NRO, NGA, NSC, INR, FLETC, DOT, BLM, TSA, NCS, SAD, IRS, ICE, CSS, UCC, CSO etc., with all their sub-departments and SWAT teams, are all more powerful and oppressive to the people now since the Patriot Act, NDAA, USA Freedom Act, and similar legislations have been passed. And this is only a partial list of these liberty-choking laws enacted in the name of security.

Now we are expecting the federal government to issue federal I.D. cards to all U.S. citizens. These are going to become mandatory. This makes no sense to me especially while we live in a culture that protects the rights of illegal immigrants by making it illegal to ask if they are citizens. Why would Americans need further infringement upon their freedoms? Will this stop illegal immigration, illegal hiring, terrorism, etc? Absolutely not.

I have worked with many federal law enforcement agencies as a police officer. In the 1970's and 80's they were very professional and I had confidence in them, but cops kept to themselves and were notably separate, and we liked it that way. We did not think that because they were FEDS, they were better than us. The federal government in modern day police training has much more of a presence and influence than ever before. Because of vast amounts of federal funding to police departments, CALEA with its oath to the United Nations code of conduct, as well as billions allocated to the same for equipment, the FEDS have unprecedented influence and control over how local police departments enforce the law. This is something new and was not prevalent during my career, especially to this extent. Every department large and small had autonomy over their own law enforcement, which is the way it is supposed to be. Today it seems we are on an inexorable path towards federalized and militarized police departments across the board. This not only invasive to law enforcement on the local and state levels, but this is also unconstitutional and creates a platform to further infringe on the rights of law abiding American citizens.[lvii] The talk of federalizing law enforcement implies the present system of policing is broken and flawed. In essence, this asserts that even though crime is down, it is the fault of law enforcement and not the fault of criminals, criminal behavior, and/or the breakdown of the social system in general; again passing the blame to something or someone other than the root cause.

The level of confidence the American public has in all law enforcement is at an all time low. The more we find out about the corruption in the FBI, DEA, NSA, DHS, CIA, TSA, etc., from drug and gun running to proven false flags such as Operation Northwoods (among others more recent) and many breeches of our Constitution, we realize our freedoms are not their priority, neither is preserving the Constitution. In fact, it is trampled upon every day and is actually becoming a bad word when law enforcement calls "Constitutionalists" and "liberty lovers" a security threat to our Nation.[lviii] This is the same Constitution we all swore our oaths to and promised to protect and which is also the root of law. To anyone with any common sense, a threat to the nation would be anyone trying to usurp or circumvent the Constitution, including government officials and law enforcement.

Today, we have the Department of Justice unwilling to prosecute the New Black Panthers for voter intimidation,[lix] which is a Federal offense. Black on white racial violence and hate crimes are 90% of all racial crimes, and the only charges brought by the DOJ regarding race/hate crime is a very rare occurrence of a white male charged with assault (playing the Knockout Game). I know I mentioned this before, but it is unbelievable to me that out of the thousands of "Polar Bear" and "Beat Whitey Night" crimes which are all black on white racist assaults, the one picked for prosecution by the DOJ was the one white person who engaged in this ridiculous, cowardly, and idiotic Knockout Game assault.[lx] The elderly and children are not exempt from these types of criminal assaults, perpetrated by blacks almost exclusively and are always racial in nature, and many incidents are caught on video by the assailants themselves who upload them proudly on YouTube. This animalistic, cowardly, and inhuman type of assault is a nationwide epidemic, and as you watch the videos, most of the suspects are laughing and continuously assaulting an unconscious, helpless victim. Shame on the media, police officials, and our political representatives for not addressing, condemning or ending these horrific crimes and for not exposing these criminals as urban terrorists. None of the black suspects have been prosecuted by the DOJ for hate crimes, which these clearly are. Equal Justice? No. Perpetuators of racial violence and hatred? Yes.

The Department of Homeland Security has recently come out with new targets for firearms training. These new targets depict housewives, children, pregnant women, and the elderly who are all armed and who are all white. This is racist and disturbing, not to mention the bigoted "profiling" manifested by our own government who claims to be opposed to such practices. If we look in the background carefully, it shows these people in their homes or at the playground protecting their children.[lxi] In other words, these are not thugs or criminals with violent intentions, neither are they terrorists, but law abiding citizens; far from the typical element any officer would have any fear of. What are they training for and why are they afraid to use targets depicting other races, ethnicities or any known terrorist threat such as Muslim extremists who we are supposed to be at war with? These targets are meant to desensitize law enforcement officers to atypical targets, not just because they are white, but because they appear to be armed and defending their homes and families. However, the fact that these targets are again, exclusively white is extremely racist in nature and is also misleading. If this was done representing only blacks as targets or any other race, it would be considered an outrage. And rightfully so.

It did happen where targets depicting the mug shots of only black males were used by police in Miami, Florida and public outrage and media coverage soon followed. The news journalists said that when other police departments both federal and state were interviewed: "*All law enforcement agencies said they only use commercially produced targets, not photos of human beings for target practice.*" In addition, the family of one of the depicted targets recognizes the threat of police having these types of images ingrained in their subconscious minds, which will in turn create a very dangerous situation for the people they come into contact with on a daily basis.[lxii] This is also true for the all-white targets the DHS has issued. Instead of using mug shots from people arrested for breaking the law, these targets are depicting only white citizens who do not appear to be breaking the law, but defending themselves. There should be outrage for this. There should be media coverage for it.

How are we to have confidence in our government law enforcement agencies when every one of them has their own SWAT team or militarized unit, including the Bureau of Land Management? The BLM recently made the news for trying to intimidate protestors regarding the Bundy ranch incident. The BLM goons were ready for battle, against their fellow Americans, dressed as military Special Forces wannabes. They only backed down after realizing they were outnumbered and the protestors were going to stand their ground. The fact that this almost turned into a shooting war is disturbing to me, based on the pretext of the conflict.[lxiii] Regardless of this, the heavy handed response by the BLM is typical of the bullying trend of the federal government. Where was this type of response in Ferguson, Missouri while Soros-backed urban terrorists were burning and looting with impunity?

The list of offenses committed by our own government goes on, even to the point of guns being sold by the Department of Justice to Mexican drug cartels. These actions resulted in many deaths, both north and south of the border and include the death of an American border agent as fallout from the DOJ's Fast and Furious debacle. When held accountable and in contempt of Congress for withholding evidence, the top law enforcement official of the United States, Eric Holder, flouts the legal authority of Congress, backed by the President's executive privilege. For those who are unaware of what Fast and Furious was, this is the best summary:

Fast and Furious was a DOJ/Bureau of Alcohol, Tobacco, Firearms and Explosives (ATF) "gun running" operation in which the Obama administration reportedly allowed guns to go to Mexican drug cartels hoping they would end up at crime scenes, advancing gun-control policies. Fast and Furious weapons have been implicated in the murder of Border Patrol Agent Brian Terry and hundreds of other innocents in Mexico. Guns from the Fast and Furious scandal are expected to be used in criminal activity on both sides of the U.S.-Mexico border for years to come.[lxiv]

So here it is revealed that our own government sold arms to criminals and allowed innocent people to be killed, to further a gun control agenda. The President used executive privilege to protect his man Holder, who was the *top law enforcement official in this country*. The same can, and most likely will, be done when a federalized police department breaks the law and violates the Constitutional, civil, and human rights of American citizens. We the People will have no one to turn to for justice and no legal recourse when this happens on a national level.

Many free thinking, intelligent Americans have come to the consensus that Holder and the Obama Administration had been actively trying to incite racial tensions and riots across the nation after specific events involving white police and blacks by failing to be impartial at the very least. The DHS also has a domestic terrorist list holding American beliefs as dangerous to the United States. Included on this list are Catholics, Evangelical Christians, Born Again Christians, Pro Lifers, "Constitutionalists" Tea Party members, organized militias, etc.[lxv] Is this not profiling by our own government? Remember, criminals profile, good cops observe. Why would these groups even *be* on a terror list? These groups comprise most of the law abiding citizens in this country, and it is disturbing to see how our government views its own people and falsely identifies them as potential enemies. Why are the New Black Panthers not on this list, especially when they make public statements such as, "We needs to kill all white people, their babies, and women."[lxvi] Why isn't the Five Percent Nation not on this list? This militant offshoot of the Nation of Islam are advocating for a coming race war against whites and support killing people of a different color than they are.[lxvii] *That* my friends, is called terrorism. Where is the public outrage for this? Why are they not on DHS targets? Where are the Presidential statements and condemnation for what they advocate? The media coverage? Silence as usual, which only emboldens such criminals and allows for a double standard for hate and racism in this country. This is all happening while there is endless media coverage of how "racist" the Confederate Flag is, even though that is complete nonsense but sets a dangerous trend to eradicate our history.

The DHS views decent Americans as a threat, yet they released nearly 40,000 illegal immigrants in 2013, without deportation and many of which have violent criminal records, including rape and homicide. Many of these criminal aliens have a "Threat Level 1" rating.[lxviii] And even illegal immigrant sex offenders are let go into the public sphere to wreak havoc among us. They are not closely tracked and are not compelled to register as sex offenders.[lxix] Since being released many of these criminals are responsible for more violence. In Texas alone, criminal aliens are responsible for nearly half a million violent crimes in a four year period, including over 5,000 rapes and over 2,000 murders.[lxx] Why are these people not considered a threat to American safety and why are federal agencies releasing them back onto the people to be terrorized again? Why do the mainstream media fail to cover this important topic?

Another startling result of illegal immigration that happens across the nation is the attack on America's children, a direct effect of our Federal Government's blatant disregard for our country's existing immigration laws. In North Carolina for example, in January of 2015 there were 518 charges against illegal immigrants alone for child rape.[lxxi] Let me repeat, there were 518 instances of child rape committed by illegal immigrants in one state, in one month. Over the past 14 months, there were well over 5,000 charges filed in North Carolina alone for child rape.[lxxii] These are just the statistics involving those that were charged for these crimes. Remember, many go unreported and undocumented. Where are the signs and protestors for young lives matter? Again, these protestors and the mainstream media are hypocrites, and fail to protest and inform the public for the protection of the most innocent and vulnerable of our society; yet they protest and riot for a violent, criminal thug who had a choice over his fate. This all happens while the American public is brainwashed into believing that multiculturalism and immigrants, who are willing take the jobs "we don't want," are benefitting our society. This all happens while our federal government and individual states give them benefits and jobs and set up welcome centers to help them as they illegally enter our country.

The fallout from open borders and the crime, violence, and drain on our economic system are subjects that seem to be off limits. Why are these taboo issues to address? Many Americans are suffering due to the high numbers of criminals entering the country illegally and committing crimes repeatedly. When they are deported, they return easily, commit crimes again, and find sanctuary in some of our cities and states that offer it. Why would we offer sanctuary to a convicted felon? Recent homicides by convicted, illegal immigrant felons have sparked outrage and have brought this problem into the public light. The killing of Kathryn Steinle in San Francisco, a sanctuary city, by an illegal immigrant/felon convicted several times, has outraged the American public.[lxxiii] And rightly so. This incident of violence is not an isolated one, there are thousands of them, but the media continues to lie and hide facts as a strategy to misinform the public about a very real and dangerous problem, while demonizing the Alpha cop who is the only entity that is on the street and ready to face this danger head on to protect the vulnerable from this threat.

The current problem of illegal immigration by those south of the border is reminiscent of the Cuban Crime Wave of the early 1980's, where Fidel Castro's Cuba dumped criminals and mental patients onto our shores, illegally, resulting in a wave of violent crime affecting our major cities.[lxxiv]

Telegram photo by Frank Decerbo

Police at the scene of Howe Street murder Tuesday.

My partner and I protecting the crime scene of a homicide.
Fallout of the Cuban Crime Wave.

Returning to the subject of anti-white racist quotes advocating violence against whites and the killing of whites, I would like to point out that this is a form of genocidal speech. Genocide is an agenda for many of these terrorist groups and individuals who advocate the killing of whites. [lxxv] According to the UN, genocide is defined as:

(Article 2) ...any of the following acts committed with intent to destroy, in whole or in part, a national, ethnical, racial or religious group, as such:

- *(a) Killing members of the group;*
- *(b) Causing serious bodily or mental harm to members of the group;*
- *(c) Deliberately inflicting on the group conditions of life calculated to bring about its physical destruction in whole or in part;*
- *(d) Imposing measures intended to prevent births within the group;*
- *(e) Forcibly transferring children of the group to another group.*

(Article 3) The following acts shall be punishable:

- *(a) Genocide;*
- *(b) Conspiracy to commit genocide;*
- *(c) Direct and public incitement to commit genocide;*
- *(d) Attempt to commit genocide;*
- *(e) Complicity in genocide.[lxxvi]*

This United Nations document which defines genocide reveals how these parameters can be compared to the ongoing racial problems in the U.S., and the overt language and actions taken by one race to intimidate, threaten and commit bodily harm (including rape and death) to another. Statistics dramatically show (as I have proven throughout the book) that this is in effect now and is advocated publicly by members of governments both foreign and domestic, Zionist Jews, the New Black Panther Party, Five Percent Nation, radical Islam, and individuals who cause bodily harm to other races and chant racial epithets such as "kill that whitey" "this is a black world," etc. This is very disturbing, and if the roles were reversed, I would also advocate against it most vehemently because it is wrong. The fact that this is ignored, twisted, and/or inflamed by the media and our own government makes it absolutely shameful. Our government loves to speak about peace and safety, but ignore and even perpetuate this prominent threat on our own soil.

Directly linked to all of this are the deception and lies we are being told while vital, true information is withheld. Here are just a couple of known tax funded government programs showing the CIA's goal to ultimately control what we believe and the way we think. William Colby, former CIA director says, "The CIA owns everyone, of any significance in the major media."[lxxvii] William Casey, CIA director from his first staff meeting in 1981 said, "We'll know our disinformation program is complete when everything the American public believes is false."[lxxviii] James Angleton, head of CIA Counterintelligence from 1954 to 1974 had this to say, "Deception is a state of mind and the Mind of the state."[lxxix] Finally, a quote from John Stockwell, former CIA official and author said, "It is the function of the CIA to keep the world unstable and to propagandize and teach the American people to hate. So we will let the establishment spend any amount of money on arms." [lxxx]

Over recent years billions of rounds of ammunition have been purchased by the DHS and other government entities which as they describe, "will be used for mass events." What is a mass event according to the DHS? The rounds purchased are hollow point rounds which are the more deadly type of ammunition and are actually banned by the Geneva Convention. These rounds cannot be used in warfare against enemies, but they can be stockpiled and used against American citizens by their own government? In what possible scenario would our "benevolent" government possibly need 3 billion rounds of deadly ammunition, if not to reach the NSA's goal? What is that goal, you ask? William Binney, a high level whistle blower from the NSA states, "The ultimate goal of the NSA is total population control."[lxxxi]

Wake up, America. Slumber, stupidity, and ignorance will not protect you.

CHAPTER 20

J.A.W.S.

Today's police Chiefs are so politically connected, enslaved, and controlled, because of the way they mimic politicians and media rhetoric in their denial of real problems, for fear of any political, corporate, social, racial, or public backlash. If you can't be a real cop and handle the position and all the responsibility that comes with it, find another profession. Cops are not politicians, we are law enforcers. I have not been retired so long that men could have changed this drastically from strong, free thinking and confident to what is so commonly seen today.

A disturbing trend in law enforcement regarding Chiefs of Police and high ranking Sheriffs is taking place in the United States. For years now the ADL and other Israeli entities have been funding trips to Israel for these high ranking American law enforcement officials in order to persuade them to adopt Israeli "tactics" for handling "unruly citizens." They are also adopting Mossad techniques to be applied to American law enforcement. Since 9/11 to 2014, there have been more than 300 high ranking law enforcement officials from all over the United States who have been recipients of this lobbying.[lxxxii] This is wrong on so many levels. Firstly, law enforcement should not be lobbied for anyone's interests, especially by a foreign entity, because impartiality can become severely compromised and corrupted. Cops should not allow themselves to be wined and dined and persuaded to use a non-American way of policing. Secondly, Mossad techniques are brutal and are not applicable for use on American streets for American citizenry. Our tried and true tactics and training have always worked in the past. Now if we look at the recent trend of police brutality, we see the old tactics are being replaced for something completely different. As a police officer, many of these incidents reveal that the cop or cops involved do not know how to handle a resisting suspect, so whatever training they are getting, it is making American law enforcement look foolish, overly brutal, incapable and/or incompetent. Even the responses at Ferguson and Baltimore were completely inept and allowed for looting, mass unrest, and violence while the police were told to do nothing. Mossad, the ADL, and Israel have absolutely no business training U.S. law enforcement. They have set an example of oppression in Israel and act as conquerors as they displace ethnic peoples and religions, build walls, and use excessive force while maintaining an Apartheid-like state; subjugating all those who are non-Israeli.

Joseph A. Walsh, Superintendent of the Bridgeport Police Department would sign his paperwork J.A.W.S. He was affectionately known as "The Boss," and that's what we called him. He became a Bridgeport police officer in 1941 and was a typical, old time Irish cop. He made many political enemies while he was Chief of police, and some of us loved him while some didn't. He ran the department his way and without taking federal money, which would have brought oversight and more control by the FEDS. Because of this, our equipment was not as up to date as some departments that had federal money lavished on them. I remember once being in a large interdepartmental car chase with the neighboring towns and when it was all over, we couldn't help but make comparisons of our cruisers with theirs. Ours were dirty, missing hubcaps, dented from accidents and from bricks used as missiles, and were overly visible with wear. Basically, our cars looked as though they narrowly escaped the apocalypse while the other towns' vehicles were shiny and new. We wore it as a badge of honor though.

Departmental service awards for exceptional duty were rarely given out to us. "Exceptional duty" was our job and was expected by our Chief, the men in our ranks, and by the public. My fellow officers and I had performed countless duties that risked life and limb, and we would not have expected to receive an award for any of them. Today's police officers are awarded routinely, for what we knew was expected of us and what we considered regular police duties, in our present society's "everyone's a winner" ideology.

J.A.W.S. respected strength in his cops, not brute force, but good old fashioned policing. Today that may be frowned upon, but I can tell you this, if you live in a neighborhood that is filled with crime and you are law abiding, it is exactly what you want and need in a neighborhood cop. But these are not the voices you hear anymore. For example, after the recent Ferguson riots a Bosnian immigrant was killed 20 miles from Ferguson in St. Louis, by black teenagers who racially targeted the victim because he was white. The St. Louis Chief of Police refused to recognize the murder as a hate crime despite multiple witnesses who told police the black assailants were shouting, "Fuck white people" and "Kill white people" before and during the attack.[lxxxiii] In this instance, the Chief of Police failed to do right by the people he swore to protect and serve. He denied the true nature of the crime out of fear of criminal, political, and public backlash. He does not deserve his position or to even wear the badge. That's the truth. This instance is the very definition of a hate crime yet it is ignored as one, which only emboldens the hate people of color have for white skin. This is just one example of how today's police departments, Chiefs of Police, and police spokespersons cowardly mimic the media and their suppression of facts and downplay or hide racial factors when it comes to black on white crime. They lie to the public and thoroughly dishonor the badge.

What a real city police car looks like.

Our Chief was different; if you were in the right, J.A.W.S. would back you up. He was a street cop at one time also, so he understood the job. Some police chiefs today would rather throw their men to the wolves for the appeasement of the public and criminals, because it is easier for them instead of siding with their men when they are in the right. On the other hand, they also do not know how to appease the public when their officers do wrong and give them the impression that nothing will be done and that cops have carte blanch to violate people's rights. A good leader knows how to do the right thing.

During my career, a Chief of Police in any department would never publicly condone criminal actions or make asinine statements regarding how citizens should act or adapt in order to avoid becoming victims. Criminals will always find victims no matter what you do. Today, chiefs have been quoted as blaming whites for black crime in their predominantly black cities. Chicago Police Chief Gary McCarthy said, "We've done a lot of things wrong in policing in this country. I'm willing to admit that…But this goes back 200-300 years to the time when Pilgrims came here and things developed from that, the African American experience in this country."[lxxxiv] *What?* With the outrageous statistics of black on black crime in his city of Chicago, he lays the blame on the Pilgrims? Amazing. Talk about "passing the buck," he passed it all the way back to Plymouth Rock.

In Kentucky a white man was shot by police after a confrontation where he rammed his truck into a police vehicle, and after it burst into flames, he fled the scene. After he was stopped, police attempted to apprehend him at gunpoint. He struggled and was shot by the police. The Nelson County Sherriff stated during a press conference, "We are glad that he is white, and we shouldn't have to be worried about that. We do not want any backlash or violence in this community because people have been misinformed," he said. "I think that the public needs to know how the criminal justice system works and what officers are able to do. And the media has not done a very good job of informing the public."[lxxxv]

A couple of points here; the Sherriff publicly stating, "we are glad that he is white," is a sad realization because race should never be a consideration when cops do their job and put an end to criminal behavior. However, this is a result of the media duping the public into believing that defending thugs, because they are black, is a good thing. The other point I would like to make here is that the Sherriff's statement represents fear; fear of mob violence and racial backlash, and when this happens, thugs will be allowed to rule the streets and no one will be safer for it. Just the fact that he felt he had to say he was glad the suspect was white, is a sad testimony to how most people are manipulated by all the racist media rhetoric. Who a police officer decides to use force on, in whatever situation that requires it, should never be governed by race or fear of backlash from the public.

Crime was at an all time high when I was a cop, the new crack epidemic had much to do with the record violent crime rate, but it did not spill out into good neighborhoods quite like it does today. It happened, but it was a rarity because we contained it. Flash mobs, blatantly open racial violence, everything you see on YouTube today would have never been tolerated. Our Chief would have sent his army of blue to crush any of that nonsense. And we would not have needed to do it with armored vehicles and militarized police either.

I never wanted to get involved with politics and I never did, but many of my comrades in the department disliked Walsh for political reasons. This is why I dislike politics. I still respected them regardless of their views and they still respected me for mine. All that mattered to the regular street cop was that he was the kind of boss that would listen to a regular patrolman. For instance, when my partner and I proposed to exclusively work with the Special Services Division as their uniformed arm and lead their raids, Walsh assigned us to this newly formed unit the very next day, because he saw the potential benefits and knew that it was necessary to help combat the worsening state of the city. I also temporarily left the Bridgeport police after I passed the Connecticut State Police test, again 18th out of 5000 applicants. I asked the Boss for an official leave of absence in case I wanted to come back. "You'll be back," he told me with a smile and a handshake. I did come back, missing the action and camaraderie I had in Bridgeport being a city cop. When I reported to Walsh about returning to work, he was glad.

"I told you you'd be back! Where do you want to work?" He knew I was a good working cop and I could have chosen any assignment.

"I'll take Red 42, with Patrolman P as my partner."

"You want Red 42? That's what I like about you, Lancia." I chose the most undesirable, most dangerous post in the city, because that is how I am built and why I had his respect. The very next day I was in Red 42 with the partner I requested.

Those who did not like JAWS were always out to get him. Take the FBI for instance. On one occasion the FBI tried a "Bait and Snitch" on our Superintendent. Here's the story. JAWS had word that a lowlife named Tony M., a convicted car thief and a man no stranger to prison, was looking for him. In fact, Tony was supposed to still be in jail at this time, so it was a surprise to JAWS that he was out on the streets again. JAWS' hunch told him Tony was sent by the FBI, so he agreed to meet him when the criminal said he wanted to speak to the Boss in private. At the meeting, Tony actually asked our Chief to reinstate a city auto-towing contract Tony's family had recently lost. The idiot then tried to give JAWS $5,000 in cash, plus the promise of $30,000 as a bribe for the contract. Walsh asked to see the money, and then when Tony produced it, JAWS arrested him for attempting to bribe a police officer. During his arrest and search, officers found a listening device on Tony's leg, and one of the police inspectors on the scene spoke into it and encouraged the listeners to come out and "join the party." All of a sudden, two government agents came bumbling out demanding the return of their bugging equipment, their money that was used in the attempt to bribe a police chief, and Tony himself. These FEDS actually accused Bridgeport officers of interfering in a government investigation! After the BPD threatened the FBI agents with arrest, they all went down to the station where Tony was booked, the equipment impounded, and the money marked as evidence.[lxxxvi] No one could get over on JAWS.

He was criticized by the political "higher ups" who asserted that Walsh had outlived his position.[lxxxvii] Because Bridgeport's crime rates were higher than most major cities, Walsh was also criticized as not being able to do the job as expected. Crime was at an all time high across the nation, so it was unfair to blame Bridgeport's ranking on our Chief. Politicians love to use statistics to suit their needs, but it is laughable when these blow up in their faces. To explain what I mean is simple. After Walsh retired on his own terms in 1989, the city's crime rates rose astronomically.

He was not perfect but he was one of a kind, one of the 'old school' Police Chiefs, and when he retired it was the end of an era. He was the last of the chiefs of a police department that would make a decision based on what he thought was right and what enforcing the law required, and never on what the threat or fallout of what the political or social repercussions might bring.

Our Chief of Police respected and backed good, hardworking old-school police officers.

CHAPTER 21

THE TRUTH HURTS: MILITARIZED POLICE

Police departments have always been considered para-military organizations, but the act of policing was always to keep the peace and the public safe; not as a military presence subjugating its people as a conquered foe.

Statistically, crime is no worse than it was in the past, and is even less now than it was thirty years ago. Cops in years past were never so obsessed with protecting themselves with all the body armor and overkill weaponry and armored vehicles at their disposal. Presently, the issue is that militarized SWAT teams are now handling normal police work, and this practice is transcending into an eventual total militarization and federalization of all police departments. Equipping as and looking the part of a soldier will make you act like a soldier. Recently in September of 2015, the newly appointed Attorney General, Loretta Lynch, signed the Strong Cities Network at the Sharia law- compliant United Nations which will allow UN troops to patrol and police American streets at the behest of our government to fight whoever our government labels as extremists.[lxxxviii] This is bad, and it gets worse with each police department that gains accreditation through CALEA, which also includes an oath to uphold the United Nations Code of Conduct for Law Enforcement.[lxxxix] We do not need and should never have soldiers on our streets whether foreign or domestic; we need good police officers willing to get back to the basics of being the good guys. Dressing up in Robocop-like riot gear with shields and batons looks like fear to me, and is no different than when a SWAT team enters a building, huddled behind each other in a line. This is comical to me, and is on the same level as seeing a cop on patrol using a Segway. WTF?

Other than the improper and inappropriate use of SWAT for duties police officers are supposed to handle, the excessive use of force and the mistakes made are numerous and deadly. A few of many examples of the atrocities committed during these idiotic SWAT raids and their overkill tactics are seen in such events as the shooting death of a young mother in Lima, Ohio, whose boyfriend was "suspected of drug dealing." Moments after entering her home, SWAT opened fire, killing her and wounding her 14-month old son.[xc] In a separate instance, a young Marine was shot twenty two times in front of his family, resulting in his death after a total of 71 shots were fired at him in his own home. He was innocent, but that did not stop the SWAT team from preventing medical care from coming to his aid.[xci]

A 19-month old baby was hit with a grenade by a SWAT team in Habersham County, GA, after an informant told police a fifty dollar drug deal occurred in the home. The child was burned and disfigured. After the family was racked with nearly $1 million in medical bills, the Sherriff's Department refused to pay. The incompetent SWAT team botched this raid on so many levels, and it only proves the dangerous mentality of a military minded police force that dress up as soldiers and play war. Astonishingly, the report of the Sherriff's Office's defense states that the parents are to blame for the injuries to their child.[xcii]

What kind of asinine training are these "special units" receiving when they conduct themselves in this way? Save your "bullet shower" tactics for your video games. Again it looks like fear, stupidity, and wanton disregard. I can question these types of new tactics because of the experience that I have dealing with these same situations; not only in dangerous raids, but in normal, everyday street patrol. For instance, on a routine patrol in the South

End of Bridgeport in the Marina Village housing project, a liquor store was just closing up, and the iron security gate was being pulled down by the owner. We had noticed a suspect sneaking under the gate with a pistol in his hand attempting an armed robbery. We immediately pulled behind him and grabbed him, pulling him out. I grabbed his gun-hand, told him to "give me that fucking gun," and disarmed him. We could have shot this man, legally. I am not saying that all cops can disarm someone without shooting them, but I have done it without firing my weapon on many occasions, whether it was a gun or a knife. So to say all cops are trigger happy and brutish is wrong. However, what I see today in the news is disturbing, especially to a cop with my experience. I am more qualified to talk about this than any journalist, politician, or jack-off activist.

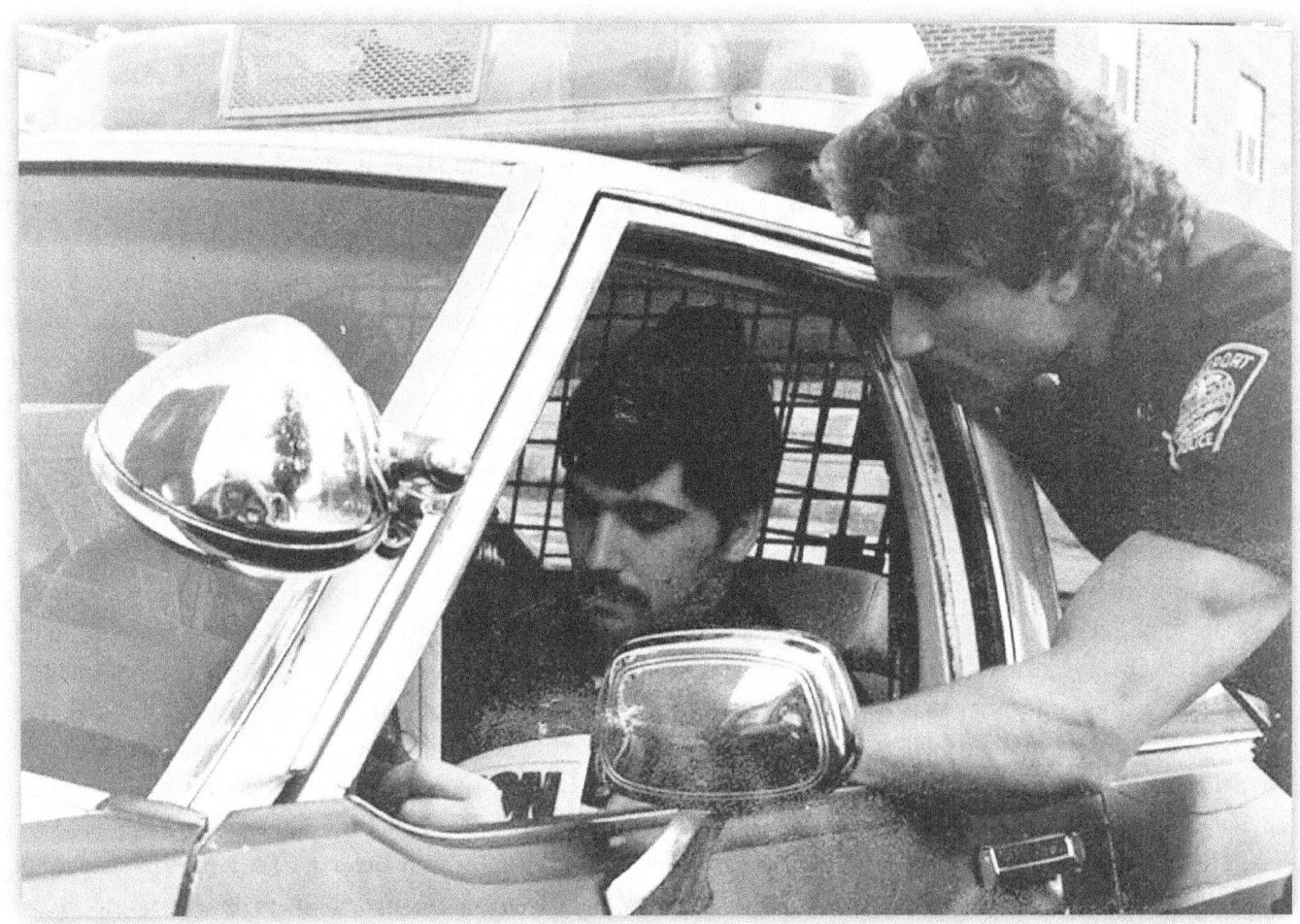

When we patrolled the dangerous South End together, there was no tougher two-man patrol car in the world.

I understand that mistakes can be made and accidents can happen, but some of these instances are nothing more than criminal home invasions made by police SWAT teams. Most of these raids are made for suspicion or petty drug offenses, and sometimes the information is provided by dubious informants. These SWAT types could never handle the situations that I, and the men I served with, encountered and the way we handled them. I rarely criticize cops in the field, but this trend is absolutely shameful. Even when I was in the patrol division we faced situations that are turned into major police operations today, and we handled it on our own. For instance, with the same partner as above, we were dispatched to a sniper situation. My partner and I, without backup, took the door down and aggressively entered the room prepared to engage in a firefight with only our service pistols. Fortunately for the armed suspect, he feared our actions enough that he jumped out of the second floor window in order to avoid being shot.

Regarding today's reaction to civil disturbances such as the many recent riots and out of hand "protests" where looters and arsonists were allowed to rampage and destroy public and private property and assault innocent people, the police were unable or unwilling to stop them even with all their riot gear and military equipment. So there it is: now we have overkill on one hand, and impotence on the other. The ineffective behavior or actions of police during these riots are deliberately ordered by Police Chiefs, Mayors, and even top government so that an eventual, heavier handed militarized reaction will become a normal sight. This type of scenario will even be justified and accepted by some of the public as the only means to law and order and some semblance of safety. In reality, we will all be treated as criminals, we will be less safe, have less rights and freedoms, and a federalized police force will destroy any confidence left in law enforcement. Should *We the People* allow our present system to change fundamentally simply because a few thugs and criminals cry "injustice" without validity?

In my career I faced every dangerous possibility a cop can face on a daily basis. I was outgunned, outnumbered, did not wear a bullet proof vest, and for most of my career carried a six shot revolver against a criminal element that had automatics such as Uzis and MAC 10s at their disposal. And we never called for SWAT. America deserves the best of the best to patrol their streets, but today we are getting men and women seemingly ignorant of the Constitution they took an oath to protect and who are physically unable to handle the rigors of effective policing. Lower IQs, fatter than ever cops, those with criminal backgrounds, the fearful, the power hungry, the trigger happy, and those with dubious reasons for becoming police officers are hired now and make up the bulk of the police departments that are supposed to protect the public. This also leads to a negative public opinion of law enforcement, and rightfully so.

Standards are constantly being eroded to cater to the above individuals, resulting in the overall public being less safe. A man named Robert Jordan from New London, CT scored a 33 (equivalent to an IQ score of 125) on the police test and was told he would not be hired because his IQ was too high. The department's rationale for this discriminatory decision was that they believed he would become bored on the job after a while and waste the training he would be given if he was hired. They are more worried about "wasting training" than with equipping an intelligent individual to protect the public and make the right decisions that cops are required to make every day. He sued the city for discrimination and lost, as the Judge decided against him and so did an Appeals Court decision.[xcii] The New London police would only interview applicants who scored between 20-27 on the test.

Jordan eventually became a security guard, so I guess the hiring standards for security guards are better than law enforcement departments. But shouldn't Police departments hire intelligent people for investigations and for solving difficult cases? Do we want police detectives to have just average or below average IQs when solving missing child cases or homicides? What if it was your kid that was missing? Backlash of stupid cops acting unintelligently turns the public against those of us who are intelligent and capable cops (my IQ is within the top 2.5%). This in turn demonizes the Alpha cop who handles his job the way it is supposed to be handled, with logic, deductive reasoning, restraint when applicable, and with an analytical mind. Good cops do not wantonly shoot unarmed men, women, or children. Good cops do not kill innocent people during petty raids. Good cops do not hurt the law abiding people exercising their civil rights in peaceful protests. But because today's hiring standards are only seeking those with average or below average intelligence, Alpha cops and good cops are lumped together with these substandard police officers and are in turn demonized by the very public we work so hard for and risk so much to protect.

Me and my fellow officers performed many dangerous raids with nothing more than what you see here in this picture.

CHAPTER 22

LUCKY CHARMS

Political correctness to someone like me is nothing short of limiting free speech, especially for those who can think for themselves. I do not need some political correctness communist commissar telling me what is offensive and what is acceptable. I am man enough to speak my mind. I do not take my marching orders from some leftist media jackass living in a politico-social bubble. I take my First Amendment rights seriously, and they will not be infringed upon.

"Ah, St. Patty's Day, another excuse for the Irish to get shitfaced," I said to my partner while we were patrolling the Downtown area on one particular Saint Patrick's Day. During the quieter hours of our shift we had fun exchanging good natured ethnic insults with each other. My partner for the evening, who was Irish, was deriding me with the most offensive, stereotypical Italian jokes I had ever heard. Some of them weren't even jokes, just insults, but we could take it. I also threw back a few good Irish jibes his way and we had some laughs.

"The streets are filled with drunken assholes," I said to my partner, "these can't all be Irish, these jackasses walking the streets drunk." He looked at me and laughed and said something about stupid Italians and spaghetti Sundays, and I laughed with him. When I was a cop we messed with each other and had fun with our cultural differences. Nowadays, you cannot look at anyone wrong without offending them. People have become so sensitive.

"Amber 23."
"23's on. Wall Street."
"23. Proceed to Fitzy's on Water Street. Reports of a disturbance. Check it out."
"23. 10-4."

I looked over at my partner and he said, "It begins." We both knew that St. Patrick's Day would definitely bring more disturbances than usual at the many bars in the city. This was our first disturbance call of the night and it would not the last, but it was the most memorable. When we arrived, loud Irish music was playing and a beer drinking crowd was outside. One bystander with a ridiculous Irish accent said, "Oh geez! Here comes the Constabulary- we kin all feel safe no'!" But it was inside the bar that we had a problem.

Ignoring the comments from the Lucky Charms Leprechaun, we entered the bar. Music was playing and people were dancing (if you can call it that), but most had their attention fixed on a man and a woman fighting. The man was about five- foot-four and skinny, while the woman was about the same height, but not skinny. Not at all. She was huge and she was beating the daylights out of the small man, who we later found out was her husband. We had to muscle our way through a sweaty throng of besotted onlookers while some of them were still dancing around us. I thought about all the good material I would have to throw back at my partner later.

We tried to separate the two brawlers to keep them from killing each other, so my partner took the little guy of course and left me to deal with "Mamma Cass." The little guy was restrained easily but when I tried to pull at the woman's arm, she took a ham-fisted swing at me, missed, and hit her husband in the face who was being restrained. The laughter increased around us while people were still dancing. When I glanced at the onlookers, a couple of them saluted me by raising their cups.

I reached for her again to put an end to her combative efforts and tried to restrain her. Normally I would take men down much faster, but because she was a woman I tried to be as gentle as possible. She pulled away from me flailing her huge fists, the momentum of which tore her shirt open. If you think the crowd had been having fun at the fisticuffs, I can tell you that after her shirt ripped open and her humongous, heavy breasts flopped out, they erupted in a cacophony of howls, jeers, and knee slapping. They were overjoyed at the entertainment we had provided them. I did not do this on purpose of course, but her attempts to resist during her drunken state caused her shirt to rip in my attempt to subdue her. I felt bad, but after she resorted to kicking, I got over it. She was angry and emboldened by alcohol and continued to attack me furiously. During this episode she managed to bite my shoulder like a wild dog, but luckily I had my police issue black leather jacket on. The teeth marks are still there as a trophy.

Up until this point, I used as much restraint as possible due to the fact that she was a woman, but now of course I had to put a stop to it by taking her forcibly by the arms and cuffing her. Now both subjects were secured with handcuffs and under arrest. I also noted that during my struggle, my partner was enjoying the little show with the same stupid smile on his face everyone else had.

We had to walk our prisoners through the crowd and back to the patrol car. I had tried to cover her over with the remains of her shirt, and on the way to the exit the husband continued kicking, but now it was in defense of his wife's "honor" because we had all seen her precious nakedness. Trust me, I wish I hadn't. Once we reached outside, Lucky Charms chimed in. "Oh, its bare-chested beauties they've got in there!" Wow, he must have really had a lot to drink. I looked at my prisoner and found her shirt wide open, again exposing her… femininity. The husband renewed his tirade when he saw his wife's exposure, kicking at us and even spitting in our direction, even though we tried to keep her covered. This prompted me to take him by the back of his pants and by the collar of his shirt, hold him horizontally like a battering ram, and launch him into the back seat of the police car. This was the only way I could get him in.

"I left Ulster to be done wi' brutal coppers!" My partner turned to Lucky Charms and told him, "Either get in the bar or get in the back of the car with him." He wisely chose to walk into the bar. Now the problem was getting the woman into the patrol car. At this point the crowd, which had been good natured up until that moment, seemed to be aroused by the physical resistance of the couple. We wanted to get this over with and quickly; it was already ugly enough. We had to stuff the woman into the back seat like a Thanksgiving turkey and she fought us the entire time, snapping her teeth at us, swearing like a sailor, and kicking. We were finally on our way.

In transit to booking, I heard some of the worst curses and most creative slurs from a woman (or any man) in my life. As I was calling dispatch to inform them of the two arrests en route to booking, she unleashed on us her verbal tirade heard over the police radio by all.

"23 on."
"Go ahead 23."

"Fuck you, you motherless sons of bitches!"

"23 en route to booking. One white male and one white female. Log the time."

It is important to ask dispatch to 'log the time' when you feel there may be repercussions for a particular arrest. Because the radio transmissions are recorded, they would have on record the verbal assault the arrested parties were unleashing on my partner and I in case they decided to make an erroneous complaint. These are just some of the things she said that were heard over the police radio while I was transmitting.

"You cops are Irish cocksuckers! You take it up the ass, you potato-faced dickheads!"

"10-4, 23. Do you have everything under control there?"
"10-4 Radio. En route to booking. Both parties are intoxicated and belligerent."
10-4, 23. Time is nineteen thirty.

"By the way, I'm Italian. Not Irish." I should have kept my mouth shut, but I couldn't help myself.

"You Italian grease fuckers!" I had never heard that one before. "WOP motherfucking meatball whores!" That's different. "Fuckin' salami makin' Guinea pieces of shit!" *Wow.*

My Irish partner, who loved the Italian insults, turned to me and said, "You gotta love St. Patty's day."

CHAPTER 23

DAMSEL IN DISTRESS

This story represents a common tragedy played out every day. Violence against women is very real and goes unpunished and unaddressed in many cases. However you paint cops in general, they are out there protecting the weak and helpless when no one else will. With all the women we have now in the media reporting, you would think they would report some of the heinous crimes committed against women and rally others to support the cause of groups such as No More, Battered Women's Justice Project, or the National Center on Domestic and Sexual Violence. Why are American reporters afraid to report vicious rape-murders committed by scumbag violent criminals when they saturate airtime with stories of criminals shot by cops? The stories of violence against women are so prominent in crime statistics that, by ignoring them, reporters are complicit in these crimes and trying to hide a fact that the public needs to be made aware of.

For just one of thousands of occurrences, American mainstream media failed to report the story of Beverly Hope Melton being raped, and then beaten to death with a baseball bat by a black male in South Carolina who then dumped her body behind a barn to die alone.[xciv] There are countless stories such as these, but yet, we are bombarded day and night with a story of one suspect who dies after a violent confrontation with the police, because the "*victim*" was black. Something is very wrong here. Wake up. We all deserve to be safe, and all true victims deserve media coverage and public support. It is racist, discriminatory, bigoted, and prejudiced to pick and choose who you want to represent as a victim while sweeping under the rug others because of their race or gender.

✳ ✳ ✳

"Red 42."

"42's on. East Washington."

"42, reports of a loud domestic dispute. Woman screaming for help. Sixteen hundred block of Sixth Street, unknown apartment."

"42. 10-4."

Domestic disputes are one of the most dangerous calls police can respond to, whether you work a big city or a small town. The area where this particular domestic dispute was taking place was in an East Side neighborhood located near some factories that were still in use. It was a low income community, filled with despair, and one of the many neighborhoods in Bridgeport that had once seen better days.

"42 on scene."

A Bridgeport neighborhood on the east side.

There were three young black females sitting on the front steps of the apartment building with distressed looks on their faces. I asked them if they knew which apartment the noise was coming from. All three females looked afraid and refused to answer. One of them, however, looked up at the right side of the apartment building, hinting to us where the apartment was located. They were afraid of something, or someone.

The hallway was dark as we climbed flight after flight of stairs, listening for screams on each landing. At about the third floor we started to hear a strange wailing sound that only a battered woman can make. Not an uncommon sound a street cop hears. We quickened our steps and made it to the fifth floor, and as the screams became louder, we knew which apartment door to knock on. I looked at my partner then banged on the door.

"Police officers! Open up!" The sounds behind the door silenced. "Open the fuckin' door, it's the police. I know you're in there!"

A male voice from behind the door answered me. "Ain't nothin' wrong here! You can go now officers!"

I looked at my partner incredulously. "Open the door or I'm gonna smash it open!"

"Mothafucka! Alright, hold on!" The door was opened and the man that greeted us was a tall, black male wearing only his tighty-whities underwear. "What the fuck the police gotta be here fo'?"

"Calm down!" I said in a stentorian voice, "Someone called and said there was a woman screaming in here, and I heard screams myself." I looked across the male's right shoulder and saw a black female sitting on a couch directly across from the door. She too was in her underwear and looked frightened. In a gentler voice I asked the woman, "Ma'am, are you alright?"

"She's fine! I told you th-"

"Quiet down! I'm not talking to you now!"

The man turned and looked at the woman. She looked at him, then to me, and with a shaky smile said, "Everything's f-fine, officer." The male then looked at me triumphantly.

"Like I said, ain't nothin' wrong here." He even had the balls to start closing the door which my size 12 boot prevented.

"I'll tell you when we're finished-and we're *not* finished." At this, we walked into the room and my partner made sure to block any exit to the door. Once the woman saw the man was no longer looking at her, I could see her appeal to me with the most terrified expression. Without saying anything she was imploring us to help her. To see this type of fear is revealing. We were all she had, and there was no one else to rescue her. I knew that he had hurt her and was about to do something terrible, and the look she gave me in that moment said, 'please help me.'

I asked the man, "Are you two married?"

"No! What does that have to do with anything? She my bitch, tho!"

"I don't want you talking like that in front of me. Don't you have any respect?"

"This ain't none of yo' business, officer."

"It's my business now." I walked over to the woman to see if there were any visible injuries. "Ma'am, can you please stand up?" As she started to stand, the man became belligerent.

"You just wanna see her in her underwear! Sit the fuck down!" he told the woman. He turned back to me and told me, "She ain't getting up for you!"

My partner told him, "Shut the fuck up asshole!"

"Ma'am, please, let me see your back." She still didn't get up because she was terrified, so I took a look myself. She had scratches on her neck, and even on her black skin I could see welts and red marks on her back. There were some old scars, too. I turned to my partner, "Cuff him. You're under arrest."

"Fo' what?" he demanded while he was being cuffed.

"For assaulting this woman, you know for what."

"She ain't and won't press charges, so take these cuffs off!"

"*I'm* pressing the charges, asshole!"

"Mothafucka, let me put some pants on at least -you can't take me to jail wi' my underwear on!" We ignored him and his request and proceeded to walk him to our waiting police car, but before we left I asked my partner to take him into the hallway and out of earshot.

"Ma'am, do you need medical attention?"

"No, thank you. I'm going to go to my sisters, she'll fix me up."

After taking her information for my report, I walked out the door but turned to her again before leaving. "He's not going to be in jail for long. When he gets out, he may want to hurt you. Can you stay somewhere else where you'll be safe?"

She nodded and looked at me with the same uneasy smile she had greeted us with. "My sister will take care of me." While en route to booking we warned him that if he ever hurt her again we would not go easy on him. He was quiet for once.

A few years prior to this incident, there was a precedent setting case in Bridgeport. During a domestic dispute, police were called to a home where a couple was fighting. The man had physically beaten the woman, and when they asked her if she wanted to press charges she said "No," most likely because she was terrified of him. The police decided not to arrest the man or even tell him to leave, and shortly after they left he killed her. Since that case, whenever there is domestic violence or even the threat of domestic violence, the abuser must be arrested and taken out of the home to prevent the same disaster from occurring. [xcv] This pertains to violence or the real threat thereof, not just a run of the mill argument.

CHAPTER 24

OTHER POLICE "DUTIES"

In this chapter I briefly mention the less desirable duties a police officer must perform as part of his tour. I personally would have been happy to make dangerous felony arrests all day long instead of the activities the "Do Nothings" reveled in that kept them out of harm's way. Different cops are built for different things. I did not like giving out traffic tickets, doing radar, handling accidents or turning off the open fire hydrants in the summertime. I am not saying these duties do not have their uses or cannot protect the public because they do, what I am saying is that a cop like me is wasted on these tasks. These undesirable tasks only needed to be performed while in patrol division as a patrol officer on the beat. When I was assigned to Special Services, Anti-Crime, and Tactical Units, we were freed from those duties to focus on the more serious aspects of policing.

I also do not like the fact that some cities and towns have quotas for traffic tickets to generate revenue. I regard this tactic as a form of highway robbery, and this is one of the reasons why some members of the public hate cops. We did not have quotas of any kind; we were just expected to enforce the law when it was broken. We also were trained in the Academy to treat people with respect during motor vehicle stops. For instance, if we pulled a man over with his wife and kids in his vehicle for a violation, we were to be highly conscious and sensitive in our actions so as not to embarrass him in front of his family, whether he was ticketed or not. Training like this was infused regularly in the Academy to keep officers aware that we were there to serve the public, not to belittle them. It seems that now this type of training is not being taught to police, which helps create a wider divide between the public and law enforcement.

In St. Louis, an elderly couple honked at an off duty police officer because they were afraid of being run into by the officer's truck. The officer repeatedly honked back at them, and when they pulled over for him, he got out of his truck and proceeded to attack the couple at gunpoint and then beat the elderly man with the butt of his pistol. When the woman called the police for help, the officers who arrived on the scene talked with the off duty cop, laughed and joked with him.[xcvi] They gave no aid to the couple despite the heinous actions of their brother in blue, who in my opinion is nothing more than a thug with a badge.

There were other duties I hated on the job. I worked undercover at times with the Anti-Crime unit, but I always refused the assignments where I had to act like a "John" and pick up prostitutes for arrest. I did not like that duty and refused my Captain when he asked me to do it. There was just something about impersonating a criminal that really bothered me. You have to really put on the air of a scum bag to pull it off. That's just not my way of policing. I liked wearing the uniform so the bad guys knew exactly who I was, and so did the good people. If I was going to get shot, I would want it to be while I was wearing my uniform. When in uniform and in the presence of law abiding citizens, I could feel that they felt safe, and it reminded me of how important my job was to them.

But there were and still are cops that live for these low risk duties and are true ball busters. Again I realize it has to be done and tickets have to be given out, but some guys look for anything they can find just to rack up the offenses. Those are the guys that buy coffee for captains to get off the streets and find any excuse they can to not engage in the real police work. They know who they are.

I always preferred hands on, serious police work. It's what kept me going. I loved the hand to hand, the gun calls, the chases on foot or in cars, bashing doors in, and letting the tough guys on the street know that I was tougher, and that if you mess with innocent people, I'm going to avenge them. You need cops like me whether you admit it or not. If criminals weren't afraid of some cops, they would be even worse than they are, and for someone who doesn't live in an area where criminals reign, they have no idea how terrifying it is for the normal people who live among them. For those who did live there, cops like me were all they had; the only barrier between them and the criminal element. If criminals are not at least afraid of the cops, can you imagine how they would treat and terrorize the people who live next door to them? It's easy to collect a paycheck and get to calls after the fact and write the report after the damage is done and pick up the pieces. Some cops know how to avoid trouble. I was the type of cop that wanted to get there before the pieces were broken.

This is why I was called off the street specifically by DEA, FBI, ATF, State Police, etc., to do the door kicking for them and to accompany them on their raids. We went after real bad guys back then. This is why I worked in the elite divisions of the department. This is also why I worked in two-man, high-crime patrol cars for most of my career. I wanted to be there, I chose to be there, I wanted to get in action every day and make a difference, and that's how you get respect as a cop. The uniform doesn't give it to you; it's what you do in that uniform that earns it. This is also why one of my short term partners did not want to ride with me anymore and requested another assignment, because on occasion I would go into the dispatch room and request them to send us on the gun calls and any other life threatening situation because I craved it. You could not work these high crime sectors and do your job the right way if you were afraid to mix it. Sounds crazy, but I also believed that if I did die a young man, this would be the best way to go. There is nothing wrong with this, because it is effective and tax payers are getting their money's worth, but being a high octane cop can also burn you out before your time.

CHAPTER 25

ABBANDONATA!

We hear so much about victims of supposed police brutality whether real or not. If you look into most of these accusations you will find there is always more to the story. The fact that most people do not realize the physical aspects of trying to subdue a resisting subject and how difficult it can be, causes a knee-jerk reaction in which usually results in the officer appearing to be brutal. Typically, the subjects of "police brutality" are not as innocent as they are painted to be by the media and by their now popular crying mother interviews. The real victims are the elderly, the young, the weak, or anyone else who cannot defend themselves against the violent element that prowls the streets day and night. They are forgotten and very rarely championed by anyone. After all the violence, blood, and despair I have seen in my career, it is the helpless elderly that evokes more emotion for me than anything else. Because of their vulnerability I can only imagine the fear they must live with on a daily basis. I have never seen anyone hold up a sign for "elderly lives matter" or "innocent victims' lives matter."

One year on a snowy Christmas Day I was working solo on patrol Downtown. At 20 years old, working on Christmas was a downer. I had many friends, my family, and of course a girlfriend and would have rather spent the Holiday with them. It was particularly quiet that day when dispatch called.

> *"Amber 22."*
> *"Amber 22 on. Downtown, State Street."*
> *"22 head over to the XX Hotel on Fairfield Avenue. We have reports of a disturbance. Screams coming from an apartment. Check it out."*
> *"22, 10-4. On the way."*

I was right around the corner so I arrived quickly at the XX Hotel which was an old high-rise building Downtown that had seen better days. It was more or less a place where people end up when they do not have anywhere else to go or people to be with who care about them. There were many elderly residing there. It reminded me of an oubliette, a place to be forgotten.

I think it was on the 10th floor where the janitor told me the screams were coming from, and he knew an old woman lived there and that she was handicapped and bedridden. I asked him if he knew if anyone else was in the apartment and he said he believed she was alone. I told him to open the door with his key, and when he did the smell was horrific. The janitor said "fuck!" and walked away holding his nose. I could not walk away, so in I went. I knew there was not a dead body there because she was screaming and swearing in Italian.

The room was bespattered with human feces. She had thrown it there herself in anger and despair. Perhaps she did it to get attention, but who could know? She was around 65 years old and had a wheelchair next to the bed. A picture on the nightstand with some feces smeared on it showed her in better days next to a man who was probably her husband in a WWII uniform. They were a young and handsome couple, both of them smiling from happiness. It was the only picture in the room. She looked at me with wild eyes, and I expected her to throw feces at me or start screaming again, but she looked at my name plate and asked in Italian and in a gentler voice, "Are you Italian?" I spoke back to her in Italian, "My parents are from Rome, but I'm American."

She smiled at me, perhaps because my Italian was so badly spoken or perhaps because someone was finally speaking to her like a human being, but her smile did not last long. She started telling me, with what I could understand, that her four children had put her up in this hotel and had left her there.

"They never visit me. I haven't seen any of them in over a year. I spent my whole life caring for them and raising them, and now when I need them they throw me away in this place."

I gestured to the walls and asked her, "Why did you mess your room up like this?" She was embarrassed and started screaming again. I could not understand what she was saying except the word "Abbandonata, abbandonata!" Abandoned. There was nothing physically wrong with her, other than being bedridden, and I really did not know what I could do for her. I called a medic to let them make the decision.

"Amber 22's on."
"Go 22."
"22. Requesting a medic to this XX Hotel location. Non emergency."
"22, 10-4, medic's on the way."

This is real life. There is no beautiful hospital room to take her to where caring nurses will all of a sudden treat her well. This is where we end up when we have no family to care for us, or when we do have a family and they don't care. Then of course if they think we are too much an inconvenience to take care of, especially when we have no money to leave them when we die, we end up in places such as this one. Lonely and forgotten.

I spent an uncomfortable ten minutes waiting for the medics. When they did arrive I asked them what they could do for her. After a medical assessment, the medic said, "We can do nothing. There is nothing medically wrong with her that would require us to take her to the hospital. Her vitals are fine; she's just a little excited. She says she does not want to go to the hospital and we cannot force her." He looked around the room. "But what's with the shit on the walls?" When I did not answer him he became professional again and looked at the old woman. "We can't determine if she is a danger to herself. Unless you want to arrest her for throwing feces, we aren't going to do anything." As they walked out the door the old woman eyed them as if she did not want them to leave.

I looked away from the door to the old woman and I told her in my bad Italian, "I will send the janitor to your room to clean it." Optimistically I said, "Maybe your children will come soon to visit, maybe today- it's Christmas."

She looked at me with a blank stare that told me she knew no one was coming. Glancing one more time at the nice picture of the couple, I realized at that moment that all happiness is fleeting. When I left the room, she started screaming again.

Merry Christmas.

CHAPTER 26

END OF WATCH

A tragic event occurred in November of 1980. One of Bridgeport's finest, Patrolman Gerald DiJoseph, was gunned down in the line of duty. He was a 33 year old veteran of 11 years. He was killed during a routine traffic stop where the suspect struggled with the officer and managed to take the officer's gun and then killed him with it.[xcvii] This happens more than you would think. He died doing his duty a block away from the Downtown police station. He was well liked by members of the department and would be missed.

Wanted posters of the suspect's face had bull's-eyes drawn on them and you can guess why. After about seven months a fugitive, New York City's finest apprehended him after a vehicle chase. We truly loved New York after this and we threw a party for the cops who caught him. The party was at an establishment in Bridgeport and we showed them a good time. The funeral, which was held shortly after the tragic event, was a full blown Inspector's Funeral with thousands of cops present from all over the Northeast and beyond who came to show their respects. Bag pipe players from the New York City Police Department added their solemn tunes to the last salute to Patrolman Gerald DiJoseph.

Patrolman Gerald DiJoseph, killed in the line of duty.

After attending the funeral I was assigned to the night shift and received a dispatch to go to a particular bar where my presence was requested.

"Red 42."

"42's on. Stratford Avenue."

"42. Your presence is requested at the Green Clover Pub on North Avenue."

"42. Um, that's way off my post- no problem, can you give me an idea what the call is about?"

I asked this because it was my presence that was requested and not my assistance. It was also unusual to be sent that far off post on a non-priority call.

"42. Go to a call box."

These were the phone boxes on telephone polls that cops would use to communicate with offices in the department when there was a non-emergency communication to be made. No cell phones or beepers back then, cops didn't use them. On the call box I spoke to dispatch.

"Jim, go to the Green Clover Pub. Officer M wants to settle a bet with some New York cops."

"What? What could they want me for?"

"Just go, Lancia. There's fucking cops in uniform all over the city getting shitfaced after the funeral. I'm sure a lot more stupider things are going to happen tonight."

When dispatch told me there would be cops in uniform shitfaced all over the city, he wasn't kidding. After a police officer is killed in the line of duty, and with the Inspectors' Funeral that follows, all of the out of town police officers who attend the funeral are in uniform. The tradition is that they will drink at the local bars in the city of the fallen police officer with other cops in uniform. It sounds crazy, but it still goes on today.

"Sounds interesting." I went.

The Green Clover Pub was a local bar in the Hollow of Bridgeport, and you can call it a cop bar. I would go there once in a while after work with the guys and would actually walk home because I lived across the street.

When I arrived at the bar, a slightly inebriated New York City cop approached me with a beer in his hand. "Hey, I like your collar pin. Wanna trade?" I traded my BPD Platoon 4 pin for his 42nd Precinct NYPD pin. I wore it on my collar for the rest of my career. This was also a tradition at police funerals; to trade articles of uniform, such as patches, name plates, tie clips, and sometimes even badges if you were drunk enough, because you are meeting cops from all over and these items are a type of souvenir. As I walked further into the crowd of blue, grey, and green I could see patrolman M who was a Mexican, a Vietnam Veteran, and a good friend of mine. He apparently had not stopped drinking since the end of the funeral.

"Yeah, that's right, come on over Jim!" The bar was packed with cops from all over the state as well as New York, New Jersey, Massachusetts, and Rhode Island. Three New York City cops were engaged in an animated conversation with two Bridgeport police officers. As I approached them, I said to myself, 'Fuck, drunken cops- nothing worse.' I shook my friend's hand, "Hey M, what can I do for you, brother?"

"Jim, we're trying to settle a little wager we've got goin' on. Our brothers from the City here think their precinct has the toughest cop in all of New York- and anywhere else for that matter." The New York cops were bobbing their heads at this in agreement. Two of these cops were good looking guys who looked sharp in their uniforms. The third however, the talker, had an amazing representation of all he had eaten that day on his shirt and tie, and he didn't look that good in his. Mr. Buffet on His Shirt spoke up with a slurring heavy New York accent.

"You 'tink dis guys tough?" he said looking me up and down with disdain. "He don't look tough at all. Your little department don't have no tough cops like we got." He belched. "We got Fornacato."

"What the fuck is a *Fornacato* -is that even a real name?" I asked.

"It's gonna be real enough for you when you see 'im."

At the time, Bridgeport police were widely known for their toughness, everyone knew that, including the NYPD who called us the Brutality Department; a dubious distinction but you cannot control what impressions people have.

M put his hand on my shoulder, "You've got Fornacato, but we've got Jim Lancia!" I shook my head at this wanting to calm this situation down. A Rhode Island State Trooper in his WWI style uniform came over to listen in. He nodded at me and took a sip of beer with a slight smile on his face. He was enjoying this.

"What are we, in high school? Come on guys why don't you just drink your beers and eat your chicken wings." I said.

Fatso chuckled. "This is like Mayberry R.F.D. compared to the City. We got t'irty t'ousand cops. You're like little girls in uniforms selling cookies." He guffawed at his little joke and clapped his coworker on the shoulder, who tried to move away from him, embarrassed. "Dat was funny, right?"

The other cop hesitated and shook his head. "No, it really wasn't funny." So even the other New York cops didn't like what he was saying. It was well known through FBI statistics that Bridgeport's crime rate per capita was much higher than New York City's at this time, we just didn't have the glamour or the exposure the City had.

I should also take a moment to tell you that I had won first place at the Connecticut State Police Olympics for weightlifting in my weight class. I trained in boxing, kickboxing, and played football almost all of my life including semi-pro, and I had earned my reputation on the street and in my department. I was pretty tough, but it was not me who made this challenge, it was the guys I worked with.

M told him, "This is one of *our* toughest cops right here! He can take on any New York Asshole, even if you do have thirty thousand of them!" You should have seen the looks on the New York City cops faces, while the Rhode Island Trooper howled with laughter at this and got the attention of a Massachusetts State Trooper. He marched over in his Nazi Gestapo- style uniform and joined our group-these guys look sharp in those uniforms. When even more cops joined us, I told them again to just have fun and that no one was going to fight. "I've got nothing against this Fornacato, we're all cops." Being the only sober one there, I was trying to diffuse the situation.

Fatso, with his belly pointing at me spoke again, determined. "You're just faggin'out, ain't 'cha? I know you don't *wanna* face Fornacato." I looked at him with his pudgy finger pointing in my direction and started to get pissed. They were determined to pair the toughest cop in their precinct with me for a fight, somehow, somewhere.

Mr. Mustard and Ketchup washed the contents of his mouth down with his beer and made sure to spill some on his tie to add with the rest of his leavings there. "Like I sez, he's the toughest cop in our precinct. We're gonna get him to kick your *ass*." Now my blood was up; this guy was not going to quit. I looked around, ready for the fight.

"Where is this Fornacato now?"

"He's not here. He's working, but we can get him."

"What the fuck, he's not even here? Well then, when you can bring his pussy ass here, we'll see who's the toughest. Until then, *fuck Fornacato*." Everyone laughed including the two other New York cops who didn't take offense any more than I did. Just cops having fun. I shook hands with all the men standing there, except for Mr. All You Can Eat who was too busy anyway shoveling down another chicken wing, and I went back to work. The fight never took place; I guess the NYPD sobered up, but we loved their department for what they did for us by catching the cop killer, and they were still our brothers. Some cops just can't hold their liquor.

CHAPTER 27

KILL SUPERCOP

Not all the people in high crime neighborhoods are criminals or thugs. We understood this, and it is what kept us vigilant and effective. However outnumbered the good were from the bad, they were worth protecting. Those who criticize what police have to deal with everyday usually live in prosperous neighborhoods with little or no crime, high tech security systems, and police departments ever ready. It is negligent to deny the good law abiding people who are forced to live in these high crime neighborhoods, because of their financial status, the protection they deserve. Defending every thug that gets roughed up during a physical confrontation with police (that the thug initiates) by saturating the media with hype, exaggeration, and edited video propaganda only hurts the innocent residents and polarizes police from the public. These are the same thugs that terrorize these people. Remember, the "no snitch" policy these very thugs espouse is used to intimidate, assault, and even kill possible witnesses to their crimes that would prosecute these violent offenders and bring them to justice.

For example, in 1997, a young black child in Bridgeport, CT named Leroy Brown Jr. witnessed a murder, and was the main witness for the prosecution in the slaying of his mother's fiancé. The killer, Russell Peeler, ordered the boy and his mother executed to prevent them from testifying. Their bodies were found on January 7, 1999 in their home.[xcviii] Thugs do not care if "snitches" are of their own race, are women or children, or if they are doing the right thing. Thugs are thugs and care only about themselves. They have no cause, no convictions, and serve no purpose except for themselves. You can hold up Black Lives Matter signs all day long to defend a thug, but if you get in his way, he will cut you down. This is the type of violence and intimidation people living in high crime areas have to live with daily. This no snitch harassment and the terrorizing of victims and witnesses into not testifying occurs more than people realize. It allows the thug culture to thrive unabated while those who live under their thumb are terrorized into silence.

This is a common sight throughout Connecticut's largest city.

✳ ✳ ✳

During my career as a police officer I have had a few street names given to me by the element in the neighborhoods I worked in. Among these names were Popeye, Tarzan, and Supercop. I am sure there were plenty of other things I was called by those who hated me, but they never had the balls to say them to my face. I guess being called Supercop was somewhat of an honor. I was given that moniker because I had earned it with how I handled myself on the street, the amount of good felony arrests I made, being fair, and the impact I had on the drug trafficking in the city. The negative side to this is that a lot of dangerous people with money can purchase your death easily with what they can offer to the desperate or to those who want to make a name for themselves.

A good friend of mine who was a prison guard in the Bridgeport Correctional Facility told me he had heard with his own ears threats against me. He also had good information from other guards that the talk was somebody was going to "kill that white muscle cop called Supercop, who works the Village." This was the short name for Father Panik. When I smiled and told him that I was not surprised and that threats like this were nothing new to me, he told me that it was no joke. It was not regular prison bullshit; the guys who were saying it were "big time and had connections." I had thanked him and told him I would look into it, but I really did not give it too much thought. Threats are a part of a working cop's life, and if you work a high crime area your life is constantly in danger, not just in normal police work but in targeted hits. You cannot obsess about it or you will not be able to do your job the way it needs to be done. Fear is a poison, and that is exactly what they want you to feel.

After lineup about a week later, a cop from another platoon, who had just gotten off of his shift, pulled me aside to speak to me privately.

"Jim, listen. I got a real reliable informant out there. I can't tell you who he is, but all his information is good. Let me just say he owes me big time. I was talking to him the other day and he mentioned something. He told me 'there's a hit out on that white cop, the one they call Supercop.'"

"Do you know who's gonna do it?" I asked. I had to consider this threat now because it was the second time in a week I had heard of it.

"He says it can be anybody who takes the drugs and cash that were offered by 'X,' who you know works the Drive in Father Panik."

"Yeah, I know who he is. Is that it? Did X put it out?"

"Well, I'm not sure, I didn't say that and my guy didn't say that. Now here's something else." He stopped talking as another cop walked by us and said hello. "He mentioned something very strange. Something about the BLA- not the Panthers, but I think whoever he heard it from knows his shit. You know what the BLA's been up to; they just took out that New York cop not too long ago. And then those Nyack cops." He stopped and told a passing cop to meet him later for a beer, then turned back to me. "Either way someone wants you gone. I'm gonna leave this up to you, but you gotta handle it. Its real, and I've got a bad feeling about it." I thanked him with a handshake and he wished me luck. He told me if he heard any more details, he would let me know.

This contract would set an example to other cops not to be so enthusiastic in doing their jobs, thus making life easier for the drug dealers. It is nothing new to try to put the scare into the police. The wave of cop killings in New York and in other cities at the time all tried to send the same message, and the BLA, or Black Liberation Army, was very active during these years hunting cops down.

So the street says Supercop needs to go. Now I took this threat seriously because a large amount of money and drugs is very enticing to the many thugs that would have had no problem killing me with the right opportunity. I was a high profile working cop and a prime target, especially with Joanne Chesimard on the loose and who had been sighted at this time in Bridgeport. My partner and I had even responded to a sighting of her on the East Side just a week before.

Chesimard, a.k.a. Assata Shakur, was one of the leaders of the Black Liberation Army, and police departments in the Northeastern states and across the Nation were actively looking for her. Back in 1973 she and two other men killed New Jersey State Trooper Werner Foerster, execution style. The BLA were also responsible for targeting and killing police officers in uniform during their reign of terror, and murdered more than 12 police officers and wounding many others over a span of about 10 years.[xcix] The suspects in the New Jersey State Trooper's killing were apprehended, convicted and sentenced to life in 1977. Just two years later Chesimard escaped from prison with the help of armed accomplices, and the police were on high alert for her as a fugitive.[c] We were itching for her capture. She even made the Ten Most Wanted list of the FBI, and the fact that she was "busted" out of prison, showed the extent of her resources and how dangerous they were.

The cop killing that the officer mentioned to me happened in New York City in 1981, and the killing of two Nyack, NY police officers responding to an armored car robbery, were even more recent. The investigation revealed that the murderers were members of the BLA. NYPD Officer John G. Scarangella was gunned down by two BLA members armed with automatic weapons. The two Nyack officers were killed during an armored car holdup by the BLA, along with a guard.[ci]

Add up the facts that Bridgeport's crime rates were higher than most of the major cities, Father Panik Village was ranked the worst project in America, Chesimard was known to be in Bridgeport at the time, the jailhouse threats and word on the street was spreading, and I was very active in making many felony arrests, my being a target for assassination was very plausible. I had made many enemies being the kind of cop I was. These people had plenty of money to pay for a hit. This is why I had to take this contract seriously now, because you never know who you are dealing with, the Black Liberation Army or just a local street thug hell-bent on making a reputation for himself.

One day on patrol in Father Panic Village, I noticed drug dealer "X" standing smugly with his entourage of fellow gorillas. I just happened to have two more police officers in the back seat of my patrol car who were on a walking detail that day, and I was giving them a ride to their post when we saw him. These cops had also heard about the hit and were angry about it. I pulled the police car over, called to the said drug dealer, and told him to "get the fuck in," which meant he had to sit between the two cops in the back seat. He hesitated, but the look I gave him told him there was no choice, so he pimp-walked into the car. His little army could do nothing, but they were pointing at me and talking to each other. One even smiled.

This was the perfect opportunity to further investigate the threat of a contract to kill a police officer, so we took a little ride to the outskirts of the projects. All the while, "X" was looking to his left and to his right, and this notorious drug dealer looked pretty pathetic sitting in between two big Irish cops. I looked at him in the rearview mirror and his eyes were opened wider than they were before he got in.

"So what do you think I told you to get into my car for?" I asked him.

"Uh, uh, don't really know, man. I don't have any bis'niss wif you anyway." He looked at the cop next to him. "Wif' all due respect."

"Oh, now you're learning," one of the cops told him.

I began to question him about the threats made against Supercop and asked him what he knew about it.

"There's talk going around about taking me out. You know anything about that?"

He seemed surprised that I knew and tried to act ignorant. "Huh?" This was a normal street reply to a cop's questions.

"You heard me."

"No, no, that wasn't me. I heard about it, but it wasn't me, I swear man! Where'd you hear 'bout that?"

"So it's true, then."

"Could be, I heard things. Crazy muthafucka's out there who'll do anything for money. Where'd you hear 'bout that?"

"Word is you have something to do with it."

"Hay'll no! Like I said, I hear what's on the street, but don't got nuttin' to do wif it." There may or may not have been a slap thrown his way by one of the cops in the back seat. "I don't know, shit officer!"

I pulled the car over to a stop on a dead end street with burnt out buildings surrounding us. I turned to face him. "So then if neither of us know, I have to assume it was you."

"Man, 'dere's brothas out there way more serious than me. I ain't saying nothin' else!"

Understanding that I knew more than he thought I did, drug dealer "X" began to shake. "So you're afraid now? You should be. Do we look like the kind of guys that you can intimidate?"

His eyes rolled to each and every one of us. "I ain't messin' wif' you guys, I can't say nothin' else- they be some scary brothas out there."

I asked him, "Do you think you can have something to do with killing a cop and just stand there on the street like that and expect a meeting like this never to happen? Do you think that I would hesitate to defend myself?" I laughed in his face. "Bring it on, asshole, we're always ready!"

The two police officers beside him also asked him questions and the answers didn't satisfy us at all. We knew he was hiding something, but he was more afraid of what he was hiding than he was of us. There may or may not have been some more slapping sent his way, and there may or may not have been the threat of retaliation if this contract was carried out. Like I said, there may or may not have been something to that effect. But I can tell you for a fact, he left our car alive and well, fully understanding that we knew he had something to do with the threat against my life, and that we were ready for it. He knew that even if they did succeed in killing me, an army of my brother officers would know where to find him and that he and those involved would need to be prepared for war.

After that day there was less talk about killing Supercop by the BLA or anyone else, but that did not mean the danger was gone. We continued arresting drug dealers and criminals, and business was as usual for drug dealer "X," only he was much more discreet and respectful. When we would patrol by in the police car, he would give us a wave and a smile. Damn right.

Supercop.

CHAPTER 28

THE TRUTH HURTS: POLITICAL PARTIES

Political affiliations of all types do a disservice to the overall political system we have in place. Instead of representing the people who voted them in, they represent a Party and give their allegiance to that party, regardless if it benefits the overall good of the nation or not. You have all failed us as Politicians and as our "leaders." We would not be in this position now if those elected officials entrusted to represent the people actually did just that, rather than what is better for the Party, the corporations who own them, or for their pockets. There are more millionaires in the Senate and the House of Representatives now than ever before. With allowing good jobs to be shipped out of this country, voting to take many of our liberties away, and perpetuating the overall decline of American quality of life, you have failed us. The people are tired of political infighting and for not prosecuting breeches of the law by high ranking officials in our government when they have the power to do so, and for not policing their own behavior. Americans do not want politicians to have carte blanche to break the law with no accountability. We must eradicate government immunity, protections, and the overuse of executive privilege. Our elected officials must be just as accountable for wrongdoing and unethical behavior as the citizens they represent. A politician should be accountable for every lie they tell. You are not royalty; you are elected officials, a position granted to you by the people.

The Constitution is still the great document it always has been and has made America what it is, but politicians such as Harry Reid use the word, "Constitutionalists" to describe individuals who are perceived as a "threat" to the nation. "Liberty Lovers" is another term for those who believe in our rights as Americans and is used to label these people as another threat. The guise of the "need" for increased security has rendered the United States a country unrecognizable to what it once was.

Because political parties are all in bed with each other and either make disastrous decisions or are completely indifferent and dishonest in representing the people and their interests, I do not personally espouse any political party. I believe all political parties are corrupt, and searching for a political party to bring America back to its former greatness is a lesson in futility. However, it is interesting to note that the ten most violent cities in America are run by Democratic Mayors, members of a political party who vehemently advocate for gun control. These cities include: Camden New Jersey, Flint Michigan, Detroit Michigan, Oakland California, St. Louis Missouri, Cleveland Ohio, Gary Indiana, Newark New Jersey, Bridgeport Connecticut, and Birmingham Alabama.[cii] How Chicago is not on the top ten list is beyond me, but this list changes every year. Restricting legal guns for legal gun owners will only empower the criminals and make these cities (and all cities) even more dangerous.

This partial list of troubled cities, and what is wrong with politics in general, only scrapes the surface of the issues that have compromised the safety of our cities and towns, which affects all of us and our quality of life. This is, to the average American, more important than any war in the Middle East or terror threat abroad.

CHAPTER 29

THE TRUTH HURTS: WHITE POLITICIANS

With very few exceptions, these entitled privileged men and women are just as culpable as the criminal thugs and their so called civil rights leaders. They use race and blaming whites to assert their agendas and to cajole anyone who disagrees with them to silence. In truth, if any whites are to blame it would be these wealthy, manipulative legislators who, against popular majority, will forcefully integrate peoples and policies that will never affect them. High crime minority areas lay blame for criminality on the socio-economic status of the community; however, no one wants to understand or admit that the cause of impoverishment is crime itself. According to an investigation in 1982:

> *"In the years between 1964 and 1975, cities in the United States experienced a tremendous upsurge in the rate of crime. The official violent crime rate (incidents recorded by police) jumped by 336% reflecting an increase particularly in robbery, serious assault, and rape (Skogan, 1978). Citizens' expressions of the fear of crime increased with the soaring crime rates such that by 1972 60% of the women interviewed in a national survey reported that they were afraid to walk alone in their neighborhoods at night (Erskine, 1974). The Strategies urbanites use to protect themselves from harm, e.g., not going out alone at night or refusing to talk to strangers, not only cost them lost social and work opportunities, but also impoverish their neighborhoods by decreasing social interaction and hence, community solidarity."[ciii]*

In other words, with the enactment of The Civil Rights Act in 1964 that brought forced integration of neighborhoods and schools including forced bussing, crime rates soared by 336%, and this rise in crime occurred before the crack epidemic of the 1980's, where crime reached an historic high. The result of which is the outrageous decline of the quality of life in American neighborhoods, all forced upon us by our elected officials, against the popular will. These are just the reported crimes, and as the study states neighborhoods generally declined and became impoverished *because* of the exponential rise in crime and not the other way around. For example, the notorious housing project, Father Panik Village was eventually demolished. HUD found homes for the remaining residents in parts of Bridgeport and surrounding towns and cities in Connecticut. The crime rates in those areas rose substantially and decreased the overall quality of life for those who were there before the relocation.

Our government knows this full well, and has recently passed and enacted AFFH, which forces American suburbs, with white majorities, to further integration via taxpayer dollars.[civ] This will bring the downfall of more towns and neighborhoods, will cause a rise in crime, a reduction in real estate value, and will decrease the overall quality of life for the residents there. "White Flight" is not even an option any longer. There's the change you all voted for. Recently, the Omnibus Spending Bill was passed, allotting Trillions to be spent on non-white immigration with full benefits and AFFH housing for those people, all the while our veterans and elderly are denied benefits, medical care and their Social Security is constantly threatened for "lack of funding."[cv] America also has a desperate unemployment and homeless epidemic for its citizens, yet housing and full benefits with work permits can be handed out to non-white, non-citizens freely.

The fact that integration had to be forced says that it was unpopular with the people, who are the ones the politicians are supposed to represent. At the same time whites are forced to integrate, the black community segregates themselves willingly with BET, black law enforcement associations, International Association of Black Professional Firefighters, Black Lawyers for Justice, black student councils, black dormitories at state universities, exclusively black colleges and universities, black news agencies, black history month, black caucus, black churches, NAACP, Association of Black Psychologists, American Association of Blacks in Energy, National Association of Black Accountants, National Association of Black Hotel Owners, Operators, and Developers, National Association of Black Journalists, National Black Chamber of Commerce, National Black Business Council, National Black Nurses Association, National Council of Negro Women Inc, National Black MBA Association, National Medical Association, National Urban League, National African-American Press of America, National Coalition of 100 Black Women, National Society of Black Engineers, Organization of Black Designers, United Negro College Fund, 100 Black Men of America, etc., etc., etc.

Unbelievably, the list goes on.

Even when blacks are supported by deluded whites who believe blacks are not fairly treated, they are told to leave a "black lives matter" meeting.[cvi] This is segregation, discrimination, and racism. The list above is, of course, just a few of the exclusively black segregated venues initiated by blacks because of their wish to be segregated. This double standard has relegated the white population of this country to a second class status and has reduced opportunities for more qualified whites simply for the color of our skin. Yet, it is never enough.

I am sure politicians profit from all of this and do not suffer from the negative effects the rest of us have to suffer. I would also tell them to stop funding overseas wars with billions of our tax dollars while pretending to bring democracy to dictatorships in the Middle East. We do not even have it right in our own country yet, and those billions would do so much good here and create the much needed jobs that you have given away so freely to other countries. You either do not care about this country and the people in it or you are completely delusional and have sold out to the lobbyists, bidding for your influence. The approval rate of Congress is at an all time low, and there is a reason for that. Many of the decisions made by our "legislators" are based on a perceived "higher level" of morality or intelligence. What does our government know about either of those?

Politicians white and black who compose our government and who are supposed to protect the people have known for years about the federally funded CIA program, Mockingbird, which influences media to report the news that is favorable to our government and/or any agenda they covertly push on the public. Mockingbird has been around since the 1950's and is still in effect today.[cvii] The CIA's Project Phoenix was another secret program enacted during the Vietnam War to indoctrinate the people, seize any opposition, and create support.[cviii] So you see this is not something that is considered science fiction, but has been done throughout our own history and are strategies still being used today by our government for complete control. Not only do they want to think for us and are, in their minds the moral superiors of us all, but they now want to control what and how we think to boot.

CHAPTER 30

"IT'S THAT BADGE THAT PROTECTS YO' ASS!"

In most cases most police officers use great restraint when dealing with arrested subjects. Most officers do not want to have to use physical force as part of their daily routine. When it has to be used, force is absolutely necessary to make an arrest for a resisting and violent person. We are all trained in the Academy to use the least amount of force to effect the arrest of a resisting party. Unless some politically correct bleeding heart criminal advocate can do the job better, this is how it has to be done. The badge and the authority of a police officer come with the responsibility of making life and death split second decisions, and most cops do not take this lightly or abuse it.

Occasionally when an arrest is made for whatever the charge is, felony or misdemeanor it doesn't really matter, cops get threatened, challenged, and called out because most criminals, although stupid, are smart enough to know that we have to behave in a certain manner if we are not physically threatened. In other words, we have to take a certain amount of bullshit on the job. Nothing new there; they know you cannot react to every insult or every threat. They sometimes push cops as far as they think they can get away with it.

In one instance I arrested a drug dealer- nothing new there either. But this guy had the stupidity to not only deal drugs out in the open (just observed a transaction being made while I was in a marked car), but had pointed his finger at us in a shooting gesture. What an idiot. I arrested him for observing his drug transaction, and upon searching him per protocol, found more drugs, a large amount of cash, and a .25 caliber pistol. I told him, "If you had any balls, instead of pointing your finger, you should've used this pea shooter. Then we could'a had some fun."

On the way to booking he had many things to say about us being "punk-ass cops" and how if he did pull that gun out, he would have, "capped our asses off."

"Yo' pigs are racist. Yo' arrestin' me because I's black!"

My partner turned to face him and said, "We're not arresting you because you're black, we're arresting you because you're a fucking asshole."

At this point I had to make an abrupt, emergency stop to avoid a pedestrian that darted out in front of our car. This saved the pedestrian, but unfortunately for the suspect who was handcuffed in the backseat, the abrupt stop caused him to receive what in police jargon we called a "Waffle Face." What is a Waffle Face you ask? In our police cruisers we had cages to protect us from the big, bad criminals, but without being able to break forward progress due to being handcuffed, the aforementioned waffle face would result when the suspect's face impacted with the grid of the cage, sometimes leaving the imprint that resembles said waffle. This may or may not have been funny to my partner and I; I do not recall, but I had to stop the car abruptly as I said. No one really wore seatbelts back then, nor was it regulation at the time.

In booking while I was writing the paperwork and he was being uncuffed by my partner, the suspect told him, "Yo partner's tough with dat badge on. Wif'out it, he'd be just anotha' punk-assed white boy." My partner looked at me and then looked back at him and said, "What did you just say?"

"It's that badge that protects yo' ass." He looked at me then and said, "Yo heard me. Yo can't do shit in here with all dese cameras watchin' yo' ass, mothafucka."

As I got up out of my chair the other cops doing their paperwork got up and backed away while my partner said, "Ah, shit." Now I wasn't really thinking clearly here and I should've taken his bullshit with a grain of salt like I did on so many other occasions, but he pushed my buttons and that gold tooth flashing at me was the last straw. I walked up to him, unbuckled my gun belt and handed it to my partner for safe keeping as protocol dictates when placing a prisoner in the holding cell, and then I motioned to take my badge off.

Pointing to it on my shirt I said, "If I take this badge off and beat your fucking ass, it won't be protecting me anymore because I'll lose my fucking job. But remember this, if I lose my job over you, I'm gonna make it worth my while. You'll regret it for the rest of your life." He knew I was serious. Street wise criminals can sense it. It's a survival instinct. I could see in his face the realization that the protection he thought he had from the cameras was no longer there.

"Don't do dat. Don't take yo' badge off please." I paused for a second after he said this, calming myself down. After all, he did say please.

"Then shut your fucking mouth and remember… this badge protects *yo-* ass."

CHAPTER 31

HELLS ANGELS

Gangs come in all colors. For instance, the many violent gangs from South American countries such as MS-13, whether they gain U.S. soil legally or illegally, are responsible for a large percentage of the violence in this country, yet irresponsibly, our government releases many hardened and violent criminals from South of the Border, without deportation. Once released, many of these dirt bags continue their life of crime and prey on American citizens. Again, the media will not touch the truth of this taboo subject, but will defend them with propaganda and politically correct rhetoric to try to silence anyone attempting to bring this catastrophe to light and inform the public.

There are telling reports of the growing Hispanic drug gangs across the nation, not to mention the high statistics of crime committed by illegal immigrants coming over the border from Mexico. For some reason, this is a taboo topic, but statistics show that Americans are suffering from this high rate of crime as well as the drain on our society. According to Kurt Nimmo of *Infowars*:

> *"The Border Patrol reported in 2010 that of 212,000 illegals rounded up in Tucson, Arizona, 30 percent had criminal records in the United States. Moreover, according to a Government Accountability Office study, on average each illegal immigrant convict has been arrested on average eight times. 40 percent of inmates in Arizona and 48 percent in New Mexico are Mexicans illegally in the country and 75 percent of those on the most wanted criminals list in Los Angeles, Phoenix, and Albuquerque are illegal aliens."[cix]*

The drain on our economic system to pay for health care, education, incarceration, etc, in addition to the detrimental effects of the crimes they commit, are the ugly side effects of an open border policy. You will not hear of this in mainstream media, and if it is mentioned there is a "PC" hissy fit backlash for telling the truth.

All gangs are a danger to the safety of American citizens, whether they are drug cartels from south of the border, Hispanic, Mexican, black, Asian, Islamic, etc., or the many thug motorcycle gangs of all colors. All one needs to do is live in a neighborhood dominated by any gang to feel the daily oppression and fear that comes with it. The elite or wealthy people in this country will never feel this type of terrorism. They would never tolerate what they expect everyone else to deal with for the sake of their false ideal of multiculturalism and diversity.

As I stated earlier I grew up in the Hollow, a neighborhood with a real mix. Irish, Italian, Polish, Portuguese, Hispanic, black, and Motorcycle gangs (yes, they are a culture all their own). There were many of them too. On the same block where I grew up as a kid in the 60's there were three major motor cycle gangs, the Hells Angels, Huns, and Grateful Dead. They were at their heyday and parked hundreds of Harleys on the streets in front of the buildings they lived in and called their headquarters. These were rival gangs who would go to war with each other at times, but the proximity of their "headquarters" actually made them neighbors. Nowadays, they are all behind gates and tucked into barricaded fortress-like buildings, but back then it was all hanging out for the public to see. On any given day as a kid I would hear the rumble of fifty Harley Davidson's with wild, long haired riders all wearing their colors.

A Bridgeport neighborhood. Tenement building
in the Hollow section of the city.

When I joined the police force veteran cops would regale us rookies with war stories of the 60's and 70's and the battles between the Hells Angels and the Bridgeport Police, along with the other gangs. They were much more active then, but they had still not faded out yet and were causing plenty of trouble.

One day I was patrolling in A-23 solo; my partner was off sick that day. I was dispatched to the Hells Angels headquarters in the Hollow because gun shots were reported to be coming from their building.

"Amber 23."
"23's on. Bull's Head."
"23. Proceed to Hells Angels Motorcycle Club on Lexington Avenue. Reports of possible shots fired."
"23. 10-4."

Bulls Head was the name of a section of the Hollow. The name has been used for two hundred years, and it wasn't far from the Hells Angel's headquarters so I was able to arrive there in just minutes.

"23, on scene."
"23, 10-4 advise."

I got out of my car and realized that I had to put on a real show of strength, because these guys were tough, street hardened motherfuckers who did not like cops. But then who did? The aforementioned headquarters was in a real bad part of town, but no one messed with these guys. The building was made of concrete block and was barb-wire fenced completely around the perimeter, with *Hells Angels Bridgeport* emblazoned on a sign in front.

As I exited my police vehicle I approached an open gate and noticed ten or so leather clad gang members. Before I could investigate possible gunshots, I would have to walk by the most vicious looking junkyard German shepherd you can imagine. He was chained with the thickest chain I ever saw hold a dog, and he was complete with battle scars to prove how tough he was. I walked right by him within his reach showing no fear whatsoever. The dog did nothing.

A big bellied, long haired, bearded member approached me. "What's the problem? This is private property."

"I have reports of gunshots coming from your place here. Did you hear anything?"

"Gunshots? Nobody's shooting, just having a little Fourth of July celebration." At this an M80 exploded in the background.

"Try not to do that while I'm standing here, alright?"

Another Hells Angel walked over with seven or eight others behind him. This one was skinny and wearing a leather vest with no shirt on underneath it, and he was sweating profusely. He had long hair and a Goatee. He looked like he had been drinking. "That fuckin' dog let you walk right past 'em as if you owned the place! That fuckin' dog bites us!"

"He's smart then, because if he tried to bite me, I would've shot it."

At this, several of the others started to get agitated and I could hear them saying things, but I could not make out what they said. The skinny guy took offense. "You wouldn't shoot my fuckin' dog!"

"No, not unless he tried to bite me. Just like I wouldn't shoot anyone here, unless you try to fuck with me."

The others stayed quiet, but Skinny chimed in again. "You can't fuckin' walk in our headquarters like fuckin' Tarzan in your short-sleeved shirt and tell us what to do!"

"I just did."

At this point it looked like there would be some trouble but I would never back down to anyone. We had a Mexican Standoff without pulling our guns for about 15 seconds, eyeing each other and staring each other down. Three more police units now arrived and Veteran cops who had clashed with the Angels many times before came ready for a fight. They had heard the Radio call that sent me to the headquarters on reports of gunfire.

Patrolman B, a Veteran of the Bridgeport Police-Hells Angels wars in the 60's and 70's, reminded everyone standing there of the battles they had back then and how many of their Angels ended up in the hospital after these clashes. Our job was done here, there were no guns being fired, and the Angels were reminded by the cops, that we were still the toughest "gang" in this town.

CHAPTER 32

MONSTERS UNDER THE BED

As much as everyone "hates cops" they are still necessary. Everyone loves a fireman, but he is not the one that will come to your rescue at two in the morning when someone is trying to break into your house and kill you. Even our troops deployed overseas have nothing to do with our protection here on our streets and in our homes on a daily basis. It is the beat the cop that comes to your rescue, plain and simple. You do not have to love cops, or even like them, but don't make them your enemy.

The elderly are a vulnerable and all too often forgotten population, and this makes them easy victims for cowardly thugs. For example, the recent story of an elderly couple married for 65 years pulls at the hearts (for those who have them) of the people who know their tragic end. At home one night, the couple was surprised when a home invader came in, shot the husband in the face, raped his 85 year old wife, and then beat her to death.[cx] How terrible for this couple to have to go through this at the end of their lives, and then receive no news coverage of it in the United States. Our media never covered this story; it has been covered in Britain by their media. So our own law abiding citizens here in the United States do not receive public outrage for the crimes committed against them and are denied public support, why? Because the suspect was a 20 year old black man. There are too many occurrences like this to even list, and many are racial in nature resulting in black on white crime, but Americans do not hear this side of racial injustice.

"Are you gonna stop farting at some point!"

"I'm surprised you could detect them through all that cigarette smoke. You haven't stopped chain smoking since you got in the car!"

"I can smell 'em! I can still smell 'em!" My partner and I were really getting on each other's nerves on one seemingly endless night shift. People do not realize the conversations that go on between cops on their shifts. It is not all police talk. That is done by actors playing cops on stupid television shows and movies. They never get it right. And I still hate the smell of cigarettes.

"Red 42."

"42's on. Boston Avenue."

"42 we have a report of an elderly woman who says her apartment was entered and she believes someone is still inside. Remington Apartments, Building 4, Apartment 8. Check it out."

"42, 10-4 on the way."

It was on a rainy, windy night that we were dispatched to a housing complex for the elderly on the East Side, not far from where the huge Remington Arms plant used to be. At one time, the largest factory complex on earth in square footage manufactured nearly every bullet used for the American military in WWII.

We arrived on scene and knocked on the door. An elderly woman answered and said, "Thank God you're here!" She was everyone's perfect picture of Grandma, with silver hair done in a 1950's style and wearing a light blue housedress, small and petite.

"Yes ma'am. What can we do for you?"

"Well, officers, I heard something crash while I was sleeping."

"It's a windy night tonight, ma'am. It could have been a tree branch or something. Do you want us to look around?" Of course we were going to check things out, but you have to talk to people this way to keep them calm in a stressful situation, especially an old woman.

"Yes please, I know I heard footsteps." We went in and checked the apartment, a clean and well kept area but we found nothing unusual.

"Ma'am, it looks like everything's alright. You must have heard something hit the outside of the building. We can check outside for you."

"Officer, I am sure someone is in my apartment. Please." Her facial features changed when we gave her the impression we were about to leave. "Please check one more time."

"Of course we will." How could we refuse this woman who was all alone and scared?

The first sweep of the small apartment took only a minute and there were no signs at all of a break-in or disturbance. The second sweep, however, was a little different. Out of the corner of my eye I saw the shower curtain move in the bathroom, just a little. I motioned to my partner to let him know there may be someone behind the curtain and we quietly approached the tub. I pulled the curtain aside quickly and there was no one standing there, but the window had been smashed. I pointed at the window and then at the footprints in the tub. My partner understood. Now we had to make a more thorough check of the apartment because we knew someone had definitely been here.

"Wait near the front door, ma'am, we need to check something," I told the woman in a calm voice so as not to distress her further. At this point, she had no idea that her window had been broken.

After every closet was checked again and even the kitchen cabinets, the last place to look was under the bed. In the bedroom was a little lamp on a nightstand which dimly illuminated the small room. My partner took one side of the bed and I the other. When I was a child, I and most children, would always check under the bed before going to sleep. There was never anything under there. Until now. When I looked under the woman's bed my first sight was of two white eyes staring back at me. He was a black male with a menacing look on his face.

"He's under the fucking bed!" I instinctively grabbed at his hand which was holding a pistol and tried to pull him out towards me, but I could not pull him out. My partner on the other side of the bed was also pulling the suspect by his foot, and so for a brief moment we had a tug of war going on. I finally yanked him out towards me and we both forcibly extracted the gun from his grip. He resisted furiously until he was finally subdued and handcuffed. While we were struggling with the suspect the woman heard the commotion and came into the room with us to witness the event.

"My God! Was someone under my bed?"

"It's alright ma'am- we got him." I was out of breath. "You were right, there was someone here." I saw that her pocketbook was on her nightstand and some of her things were pulled out of it. "Did you have any money in your pocketbook?"

"Yes sir, I have twenty-five dollars in there." After she checked the contents she cried out, "It's gone!"

Knowing the suspect had rifled her belongings and taken what little money she had, I searched his pockets and pulled out a wad of bills, which I proceeded to shove under his nose. "Steal from an old lady you piece of shit?" I turned to the old woman. "Ma'am, here's your money."

"Oh, but some of this isn't mine. There's more than twenty-five dollars here."

The black male spoke up. "Some o' dat's mines!"

"You got a lot of fucking nerve speaking up- excuse me ma'am." I turned to the woman again and said, "Use the rest to pay for the window this asshole broke. I'm sure he's willing to pay for it."

"Hell no, mothafu-" I may or may not have slapped him to shut him up. Before we left with the suspect we told the woman to call maintenance to fix the window and that if she had any family, to call them so she would have someone to stay with her that night. We assured her she could call the police again if she felt the need for it. "No one's gonna hurt you now, Ma'am. We're taking him to jail."

"42's on. En route to booking. One black male. Suspect arrested for breaking and entering during night hours; was still in the apartment. Suspect was armed."

"10-4, 42. Is the complainant in need of medical assistance?"

"Negative radio, she is fine, I advised her to contact maintenance to fix a damaged window, the point of entry."

"10-4, 42- good work."

Immediately after I got off the radio, I turned and looked back at the suspect.

"You're lucky you're still alive you piece of shit! A fucking gun for an old lady? You fucking punk! What were you gonna do with that gun hiding under her bed? You're gonna do time for this one. If you ever go near that old woman again I will hunt you down and there's nowhere you'll be able to hide. Do you understand that?" He nodded with a blank stare. He knew I meant business.

I sometimes think about the old woman and what would have happened to her if we did not do a second sweep or take her seriously. I truly believe God protected her and used us to do it.

Sometimes, when you look, there *are* monsters under the bed.

CHAPTER 33

THE BABY CALL

Every day, cops handle human interest situations that go unnoticed but are highly relevant to the people we serve. A good cop, even when ordered to do something they know is wrong, will always choose instead to do what is right. Police officers should not be automatons.

As a point of historical interest, the Bridgeport Police Department was the first department in New England to have radio communications featured in their patrol cars.

Calling in to Dispatch.

The members of Dispatch or "Radio" were manned by other police officers when I was a cop. Nowadays, most departments have civilians handling the transmissions. Sometimes, in a police department that was as busy as Bridgeport was in the 80's, dispatch could be a little forgetful of priorities when they were deploying so many vehicles to so many places. Sometimes you had to remind them what those priorities were. All conversations between radio and police vehicles are recorded.

"Green 31."
"31 on. Berkshire Avenue."
"31. Proceed to the 3000 block of Boston Avenue. Meet the father of a missing child. Description of child is a four year old black female last seen wearing a yellow dress. Render assistance."
"31. 10-4, on the way."

I was working solo that day and as I pulled up to the location, I met a black male on the corner. When I approached him I realized he was a friend of mine. We had trained together in kickboxing and he had taught me well. He was a good guy.

"Jim! I'm glad it's you, man! My daughter's missing."

"Get in the car, C. We'll find her." He hopped in the front seat. He looked worried as I asked him where his daughter was supposed to be.

"I don't even know, she's supposed to be at home. I just got back from work and no one was there. My wife's sister was supposed to babysit."

"Where's your wife?"

"She's working, I guess. She's a nurse at Bridgeport Hospital."

"Where does the sister live?" I asked him.

"She lives out of town, I called but nobody answered." C was really nervous but he tried to conceal it. I drove him around the neighborhood and as we were searching, we tried brainstorming to try to figure out where she could have gone off to or who she might be with. While we were discussing possibilities, I was interrupted by a Radio call.

"Green 31."

"These assholes do *not* leave me alone," I told C.

"31's on. Boston Avenue."
"31. Proceed to Yale Street on a car alarm."
(Pause.)
"31 Do you read?"
"31- I'm on this missing child call, we still haven't found her."
"31. Proceed to the car alarm call."

"Oh my God, you gotta go somewhere else now? How am I going to find my daughter?"

"C, don't worry. I'm not going anywhere. Watch this."

"31- I have the father of a missing child with me in my vehicle. His child, a four year old girl, is missing, and we are actively searching for her. If you want me to respond to a car alarm and disregard this missing child call, I will do

as ordered, but I want the time documented and I want to hear you tell me again- to leave this father, whose child is missing, to go and handle a car alarm."

(long pause.)

"Negative 31. Stay on the Baby Call. I repeat. Stay on that Baby Call. The time is 1523. Stay on the Baby Call! Respond 31- Acknowledge!"

"31. 10-4. I will keep you updated on the status of this missing child."

Even in his state of worry, C laughed at Dispatch's response.

Approximately fifteen minutes later, and to the father's relief, we found the child safe and sound. The mother, who had left work early that day, had taken their daughter to her grandmother's for a visit. We saw them getting out of the car that his wife had just parked in front of their building. In a day before cell phones, miscommunications happened often. Father and daughter were reunited and everyone was safe and happy. A rare good ending.

CHAPTER 34

BULLY BEAT DOWN

On routine patrol in Father Panik in a green and white, we encountered a suspect who we knew had warrants on him for assault and robbery. He was walking with a Doberman on a leash beside him. As we approached him, he looked as if he wanted to run but he didn't. I said, "Nice dog." Maybe he thought we were just going to talk and shoot the breeze with him, so he decided to be cocky.

"I know it's a nice fucking dog."

"Now is that how you reply to someone who's giving you a compliment?" I asked. I then questioned him on his name. He didn't respond but decided to make a run for it. We ran him down, and my partner and I quickly subdued him. He tried to struggle, but there were two of us and we were able to keep him from hurting himself. His dog ran off. Good. Let Animal Control take care of him, he's probably better off.

Downtown Headquarters holding cells. These would all be filled on a busy night.

We transported the suspect to booking, pulled his record, and found that he was a boxer with a long rap sheet of assaults, robberies, and other not-so-nice charges. The very definition of "thug." The warrant he was arrested for was for a robbery and assault on an elderly woman. When I looked over his record I showed it to my partner and shouted over to the holding cage where the suspect was detained.

"What a hero. You're wanted for robbing an old woman and taking her hard earned Social Security check. What a tough guy!" He returned my comment with a menacing look that made him look uglier than he already was. The booking officer told the suspect to take his belt and shoelaces off; as was standard procedure so they could not be used as weapons or to hurt himself with.

"Go fuck yo'self, you pasty white punk ass pig." This particular officer was pasty, I'll admit, because he worked inside a lot, but he was a good guy and just doing his job. I asked this officer to open the holding cell so I could ensure the suspect complied with protocol since he wouldn't voluntarily relieve himself of shoelaces and belt. The cage was opened.

The suspect stood there like the dumbass he was. I looked down at his shoes and pointed. "Take off your shoelaces." Taking my eyes off him for one second was a mistake. He took his best shot at me and hit me in the jaw, a jaw God forged with iron. I was surprised at being hit, and he was surprised that I didn't go down or even move an inch. Before I had time to think, he tried it again. This time I was ready and used everything my fists had to beat this asshole down in order to subdue him because he was fighting hard. There were other cops in the booking area, and seeing another officer in a fight, they instinctively wanted to help me. Officer N, who was a good friend of mine, actually held the other cops back, seeing that I was handling the situation myself. "Let him do it on his own. He wants it that way," he told the others. I was glad he did that. I took this asshole down myself with my fists, boxer to boxer. The good guy won. Afterwards, I looked in the mirror and saw that he had cut my jaw with his sucker punch. I came out and yelled at him, "You piece of shit- look what you did!"

"But look what yo' did to me!" Both of his eyes were blackened and swollen almost shut, and his nose was bleeding. "Yo' kicked my ass."

"That's right I did," I told him after seeing the results of our match. He grunted at this and nodded at me.

"Alright. Yo' the toughest cop…in *dis* department!"

CHAPTER 35

THE TRUTH HURTS: THE SCHOOL SYSTEMS

A large portion of our tax dollars fund public school systems, where the children of this country are supposed to be educated and given the necessary tools to prosper in life. The funds are dedicated to education, but instead of learning the essentials for building young minds, they are fed biased and propagandized curricula and are being indoctrinated with a "white guilt" trip, revisionist histories, and elements of Critical Race Theory. This theory teaches that, if they are white, they are to blame for the "plight" of the black race; beginning at the birth of the nation to the "social ills" of today. This false ideology gives the impression that the white male police officer, and all he represents, is the enemy and one to be hated. In addition, as a result of these teachings, white children are being beaten and bullied by the very blacks and minorities that are being told that white skin caused their grief. This is tantamount to teaching hate. Add this with evolutionary theories, teaching homosexual and bisexual agendas contrary to the majority Christian population and their beliefs, and you have allowed and perpetuated the moral decay of the most innocent of our population.

This bullying and abuse extends to the faculty as well. Recently, a Cincinnati public school teacher, Pamela Bullock who is black and works with disabled children, was confronted for her abuse of a white, non-vocal disabled student. She threw things at him, hit him, mocked him, and made racist statements such as, "Anything else, your highness? … My people fought for years, so we wouldn't have to serve white people like you."[cxi] For all this, she "resigned" from her position and the mainstream media did not cover this story to any notable extent. Where would someone in a position of teaching our children get this type of hatred, and direct it towards the most innocent and vulnerable of her students? This woman is a thug.

Universities are pushing hateful, racial agendas which demonize the Founders of this country and are attempting to completely change history. Their revised versions include white male Christians as everything that is wrong with society, from the birth of the nation to the perceived racism of today. Mexican professor at Texas University, Jose Angel Gutierrez says, "We have got to eliminate the gringo, and what I mean by that is if the worst comes to the worst, we have got to kill him."[cxii] Jewish professor Noel Ignatiev from Harvard University is on a campaign to eliminate the white race, saying, "Make no mistake about it: we intend to keep bashing the dead white males, and the live ones, and the females too, until the social construct known as 'the white race' is destroyed—not 'deconstructed' but destroyed."[cxiii] His inciting, genocidal speech continues with, "Abolish the White Race- by any means necessary."[cxiv] These are not isolated incidents, but are perpetual and more common than most people realize.

Jewish author Howard Zinns' book and blatant revision of history, *A People's History of the United States* blames whites for all of humanities ills, and is taught as fact in many universities despite the criticism his work has received by scholars and historians. Zinn twists the truth to show whites as the central oppressors of everyone across the board.[cxv]

Other college professors are also pushing this white genocide agenda. Kamau Kambon, professor of "African American Studies" said this: "And then finally I want to say that we need one idea, and we're not thinking about a solution to the problem … And the one idea is, how we are going to exterminate White people because that in my estimation is the only conclusion I have come to. We have to exterminate white people off the face of the planet." And Haunani-Kay Trask, a professor of Hawaiian Studies feels this way, "Racist White woman I could kick your face, puncture both eyes. You deserve this kind of violence."[cxvi] Vanderbilt professor, Tony N. Brown, blames the Baltimore riots of 2015 on "White Privilege," and not on the thugs that are actually committing the criminal acts. He speaks out against all whites, delivers blanket racist statements about white parents and ignores the majority of criminality belonging to the black culture and the failure of black parents. His statements, as well as those made by others blaming whites for working hard and achieving throughout the centuries, is in retaliation for the death of the glorified thug Freddie Gray. He calls for the surveillance of white people to better monitor their behavior towards blacks.[cxvii] This is not only an asinine statement made by a complete ignoramus, but before the recommendation for monitoring whites, as he ridiculously suggests, he needs to look to his own people who are committing most of the violent crimes on record and have made our streets so dangerous and uninhabitable that civilized people, of all races, want to distance themselves from them.

So Brown suggests a nationwide "monitoring of whites?" Let's dissect this. This suggestion was made because of supposed racism, profiling, and discriminatory practices by the police. Brown's prescription for this is to discriminate against and racially profile whites to monitor them. What kind of PhDs are they handing out that would allow anyone to make such a hypocritical and racist statement?

The fact is, there is no white privilege, which was a farcical theory to begin with. There is only black and minority privilege. This privilege not only allows them to get away with vile, racist statements made publicly, but also gives them a platform to do it in our schools and Universities while being paid a salary, which would not be tolerated if similar statements were made by whites against blacks or any other race and culture. Interestingly, one of the originators who helped coin the phrase "white privilege," David Ruenzel, who was also a writer for the Southern Poverty Law Center and champion for the black race, was killed by two black suspects while jogging in his Oakland neighborhood. His "white privilege" did not protect him from the very people he advocated for.[cxviii] It is ironic that the very term white privilege which causes hate and outrage, if it is believed by the simple minded to actually be true, can perpetuate the very violence that ended Ruenzel's life.

The list of racism and genocidal threats against whites continues, which in turn clears a direct path towards hating anyone who is white and especially one in a power position, such as the white police officer. It continues to flow to every white member of society, but we fail to ask one important question. When whites are "bred out" and eliminated, who is next? The Asian? The light skinned Hispanic? Food for thought.

Why should anyone, white or otherwise, accept a genocidal wave of speech resulting in crime and violence that directly targets them? It is interesting that only countries that are dominated by whites are being flooded purposely with minorities. Again, there is an agenda here, cloaked in words like "diversity" and "multi-culturalism," but instead of focusing on what is really important, which is not preaching hate regardless of color, the public decides to take up the cause of minority thugs, illegal immigrants, and Islamic "refugees" who are criminals. After taking up these ridiculous causes, the public then turns around and blames their "plight" (criminal behavior) on anything other than its true cause. Our society has focused on minorities in general with tax dollars, programs, affirmative action, minority loans, and other programs such as welfare and what HUD provides, and nothing has become any better, even under the Totalitarian reign of a black President.

The racist bashing of whites goes beyond Universities and schools and takes a lead role in the media. Jewish anti-white Arthur Sulzberger Jr., owner of the New York Times, knows the game he is playing when censoring news stories. He says, "If white men were not complaining, it would be an indication we weren't succeeding and making the inroads that we are."[cxix] Again what becomes normal and practiced on a regular basis in the media floods into every aspect of society, and is repeated over and over, in every institution, until it is accepted. But why are we accepting this?

CHAPTER 36

"YOU CAME CLOSE TO DYING TONIGHT"

"Amber 23."
"23's on. Golden Hill Street."
"23. Head over to Flannigan's on Fairfield Avenue. Altercation between a while male and a black male. Black male is armed with a knife. Any other vehicle in the area, can you respond?"
"23. Right around the corner."

✳ ✳ ✳

"23's on scene."
"10-4, 23. Time is twenty-one hundred.

Before we exited the vehicle and pulled up in front of the bar, we observed a black male carving up a white male like a thanksgiving turkey. If we had not arrived when we did, the victim would definitely have been killed. The black male did not stop stabbing him until we yelled out to him. I would have shot him at this point, but he was too close to the victim and there was no clear shot.

"Put that knife down motherfucker!" He turned around, saw that we were cops and started running. My partner stayed with the badly injured white male to render assistance and I gave chase on foot through the downtown streets. I have been in many foot chases before, but this one was odd because he had committed a serious assault or possible homicide and did not drop the knife. I could still see it in his hand because I was no more than 25 feet away from him at any given time. I was running with my gun drawn also, and I did not know if he was going to try to use the knife on me. During the chase at several points I felt that I should shoot him, but I didn't, because I never felt threatened enough to fire.

He did not seem to be tiring at all, and I was not going to keep running with him holding that knife, so I yelled out to him about 20 feet away, "Drop the knife now or you will be killed." He stopped and turned still holding the bloody knife as my gun was pointed right at his chest. He decided to drop the knife a fraction of a second before I pulled the trigger. I did not need to shoot him now. "Drop to the ground away from the knife, hands behind your back." I stepped on his neck with my foot. "If you make any moves, I will kill you." He didn't make any moves and I cuffed him, took the knife as evidence, and walked the long walk back to the vehicle.

The ambulance at this point was on scene, and my partner told me the victim was unwilling or too weakened by the multiple stab wounds to talk about the reasons for the fight. For someone who had been stabbed as badly as he was, he took it pretty well and he was still coherent. "You got here just in time, I couldn't take much more," he said as he grimaced in pain. The medics on the scene agreed with this and, out of earshot of the victim, advised me his injuries were life threatening. They rushed him to the hospital with their sirens blaring, and we transported the suspect to booking.

"23's on."

"Go 23."

"23, Medics have rendered assistance to injured party- victim of a serious stabbing, Assault One. They are en route to Park City Hospital. We are en route to booking-one black male."

"10-4, 23. Twenty one twenty."

I turned around and faced the suspect sitting cuffed in the backseat. "Right now you're being charged with first degree assault, maybe attempted murder, and if he doesn't make it, it will be murder. Oh by the way, it's good you dropped that knife when you did, you don't know how close you came to dying tonight."

CHAPTER 37

THE PRIDE OF THE BRITISH NAVY

Downtown Bridgeport is no safe place to be at night. There are a few decent restaurants there, but you cannot wander too far from them. There are also plenty of bars Downtown, but I wouldn't recommend patronizing them, day or night, unless you are looking for trouble. The city had its heyday, but that is long gone.

✳ ✳ ✳

"You gonna eat that sandwich sometime soon or are you gonna take it home and make love to it?" My partner had a huge chicken parmesan grinder on his lap, which looked tasty, but it was making the car smell like a Sicilian whorehouse.

"When we get ten fuckin' minutes of peace, I'll be able to finish it off like a human being-and don't be eye-ing' my sandwich, Jim, you eat like an animal." It was a busy night and my partner was a slow eater. I had already pounded down my sausage and peppers in just a few minutes.

"Oh, look at this! These fucking assholes are bitch-slapping each other in front of the hotel! No wonder why nobody wants to come to this town." After glancing at the two parties in question, my partner carefully re-wrapped his sandwich and placed it lovingly in the glove compartment for safe keeping.

"Red 42's on."

"Go 42."

"42. We're checking out a disturbance between two ladies of the evening in front of the M Hotel, Downtown."

"10-4, 42. Time is twenty-ten."

Now when we say "ladies of the evening," we use the term loosely. On any given night in downtown Bridgeport you may see some prostitutes who are actually women, but for the most part, you will see prostitutes that dress only to try to *look* like women. There are certain aspects about men that a dress, a wig, and lipstick just cannot hide.

"Oh my God," My partner said, "The one on the right looks like Carl Weathers in drag!" We laughed as we got out of the car.

"Alright!" I told the 'girls.' "Calm down, there's decent people trying to walk into this hotel here!"

At the sight of cops, the 'ladies' stopped slapping each other for a moment and turned their attention to us. One of them did not realize her blonde wig was askew. "Dis ho' be comin' over here to 'dis classy-ass hotel tryin' to hustle my mens!"

"Bitch who you callin' ho,' you don't own this hotel!"

We had to let them talk so we could find out what the problem was, not that it mattered. I'll admit it was a little entertaining, but it gets old fast. A nice couple walked by and was trying to enter the hotel after dining out. They were obviously not comfortable with the local flavor, and were very happy to see the police on scene.

"Move aside for these people and let them pass." I told the 'girls.' "Now first of all, it's illegal to solicit sex for money, I know you know that."

"Weel, I don't know nothin' about that, we just walkin' here."

"But you just told me this one was working your territory and taking your customers."

"No one said nothin' about customers, we just want to meet some nice mens for a date. Ain't nothin' wrong with that." The two seemed to be friends again and banded together in their denial.

"Well, go somewhere else and argue. I don't want to see you back here; if I do, I'll arrest you on prostitution charges." I had had enough of these two.

"Okay, Awfissa!"

"42's on. Dispute settled, both parties sent on way."
"10-4, 42. Time is twenty-twenty three."

We walked back to the car and my partner reached directly for the glove compartment with a stupid, hungry grin on his face. But before he could take his sandwich out, he noticed something.

"What the fuck is walking this way?" When I looked in the direction my partner was looking in, I saw approximately ten men parading towards us dressed in all white, a very strange sight indeed walking Downtown. "Is the Circus in town or something? Sailors- They look like sailors, yeah, they're wearing those sissy- white uniforms."

"They don't look American," my partner told me. They approached us intent on asking us a question, and the accent they had let us know they were British. They told us that they were sailors from the Royal Navy and their frigate had docked in Bridgeport Harbor. They were on shore leave and wanted a place to go to continue their drinking. They were a jolly group of fellows, already a little tipsy on whatever those Brits drink. They all asked where the "best drinking holes" were and I gave them good advice. "Listen *mates*, whatever you do, you're not going to find anywhere worth going to in this area."

"Oh come now, it ain't all that bad!" He pointed at the two prostitutes who I had just sent on their way. The two 'ladies' had stopped, turned, and were watching the group of potential customers with interest. "There's two lovelies now!" Now I knew they were already drunk.

I wanted to warn them, "Listen guys, you do not-" Ah, forget it. I didn't have the energy.

"It ain't New York, that's for sure," barked a pencil-headed sailor, who was all teeth, with a Cockney accent, "but there's got to be something worth our while in this crap-hole." They all laughed at this sailor's wit. Very funny.

"Yeah, right. You can get drunk down here, and you can also get laid-but your dick might fall off later." I looked at the one who seemed to be in charge, a pie-faced, pasty Brit. "It's pretty dangerous down here, especially for guys dressed in all white."

They laughed again and said, "They'd be dealing with the British Navy, Copper. Besides, there are ten of us; we can handle double our number in Americans!" Another man joined his friend and said, "Yeah, our dicks ain't falled off yet!"

They laughed again and I laughed with them because I knew they didn't stand a chance. I pointed to several drinking establishments and told them good luck. They left laughing and slapping each other on the back. Not even an hour went by and we received a call from dispatch.

"Red 42."

"42's on. East Washington Avenue."

"42. Head over to Doyle's Bar on Broad Street. Report of a large confrontation and disturbance. Any other vehicle in the area able to provide backup for 42?"

"42 on the way."

Low and behold, the pride of the British Navy were bloodied and battered when we arrived on the scene. The battle was over by the time police arrived, and it seemed they did have to handle double their numbers in Americans after all, but it looked as though they had gotten their asses handed to them. I approached Pie Face and said, "I told you this isn't the place to go." I looked around to see the extent of injuries; nothing more than fat lips, swollen eyes, ripped uniforms, and some bloody noses. "Anyone need a medic?"

"Nothin' we can't handle, Copper. We can get bandaged up at our own infirmary."

"So what happened?" I asked.

"A few of your colored Yanks apparently didn't like our dress. We don't take kindly to insulting our uniforms."

I laughed. "Did you give as good as you got?"

"Well, you don't see them chaps here, now do ya?"

"I'll admit you stood your ground."

He appeared more sober now, as were the others who could still stand up. Before they headed back to their ship, he turned to me and said, "Shoulda' taken your advice, Copper. All in good fun though. Won't be coming back to this shitty place again." They were not laughing this time.

CHAPTER 38

"THE MAN'S KILLING MOMMY!"

The pretentiousness of the media and of the people in public light never ceases to amaze me. They throw out judgments and accusations based on asinine assumptions and propaganda all while imprinting their couches with their fat asses, inside their safe and secured homes. Toni Morrison, a black female octogenarian from England and winner of a Nobel Peace Prize as well as a Pulitzer Prize, made this ridiculous statement about American police. "I would like to see a cop shoot a white unarmed teenager in the back and charge a white man for raping a black woman."[cxx] Wow. Do they give these prestigious awards to just any Jackass? First of all, do you really want to see *any* teenager killed for the sake of a stupid, uneducated statement? In addition, her indignation of wanting to see a white man charged with rape of a black female is based on what? The fact is that interracial sexual assault is almost exclusively black on white. There are almost no documented instances of white on black rape.[cxxi] In fact, if Toni Morrison only did a little research she would find that in 2005, for example, 37, 460 white women in the United States were raped or sexually assaulted by black males, while in the same year, between 0 and 10 black women were raped by white males.[cxxii] Toni Morrison is simply a racist who is making racist, ignorant, and insensitive statements while hiding behind her "prestigious" awards.

"What's the file number on that?" My partner asked as he was finishing up paperwork from the last call we were on, a burglary on the East Side. It was a summer afternoon, and we were still in our police cruiser and parked in front of the Downtown Police Station. My arm was leaning out of the window when I felt a touch on it. It surprised me, and as I looked over, I saw a little black hand grabbing at my bicep. It was a young girl, around nine years old and looking terrified.

"The man's killing mommy! Can the police come?" She released my arm and pointed at a car parked on the corner. We could now visibly see some type of a commotion inside the car. We immediately exited our cruiser and approached the vehicle on a run, where I noticed a large black male striking a female with very heavy punches.

I reached the vehicle first, opened his door, and pulled him off of the woman before he could do any more damage. He wasn't finished throwing punches though, and he threw a few at me. My fist to his face stopped him short and sent him sprawling to the ground. He still wasn't finished, and before I could cuff him, he tried to run away from me. I tackled him in the middle of the street before he could get too far. My partner came to assist me, and we were finally able to get the enraged man handcuffed, but not without a struggle.

"How's the woman?"

"She's messed up, he would've killed her." As I was walking the suspect back to the patrol car, I got on my hand radio.

"Red 42's on."

"Go 42."

"42, Send a Medic in front of Headquarters on Congress Street. Female in need of medical attention, severe trauma to the face and head. We have a suspect in custody."
"10-4 Red 42. Medic Two, Priority."
"Medic Two on, we copy that. On the way to that location."
"10-4, fifteen hundred hours."

As I was placing my prisoner in the back seat of the police car, my partner stayed with the woman and the child, who was now crying at the sight of her mother's mangled face. We were waiting for the medic to arrive as I was standing outside the vehicle, trying to collect myself after the physical confrontation. A Jeepload of college aged white kids pulled up about thirty feet past me and stopped their vehicle, stuck their heads out of their windows, and heroically called out, "You racist pig!" I was astonished, and even a little confused. I started to approach the vehicle to see what their problem was, but as they drove away they yelled, "No wonder why you're hated! We saw you beat that black man, you piece of shit cop!" Now I ran towards the vehicle, completely enraged, and they accelerated and sped away.

This is what you get for saving the life of a black woman. The idiots in the Jeep, to me, represent the brainwashed elements of the public; they see only what they choose to and ignore the truth of a situation that was handled the only way it could have been. They are also representative of the weak white people that hold up signs at protests saying, "Black Lives Matter" and ignore the lives of everyone else- as if white, Asian, Hispanic and all other lives do not matter. They only show these signs when a black person is killed by a white cop, and never for the thousands of blacks who are killed by black thugs, or for the thousands of innocent whites also killed by black thugs. That's because they are hypocritical, weak and willfully ignorant while they worship the black male thug culture. All anyone has to do is look at the statistics and use common sense.

The suspect I had in my custody was stopped before he could kill a little girl's mother, and he was in much better shape than she was after we arrested him. This was a first class arrest, but because you are winning a fight, doing your job, and you are white and the suspect is black, you are the oppressor no matter what. This is the hypocrisy cops constantly have to deal with. The politicians, race baiters, the ignoramus public, the media, and everyone else will deny this happens, hide it, or excuse it because it does not serve their political or social agendas. We were used to it, though; this was not the first time it happened, nor was it the last, but it does wear a good cop out over time. When I looked at that woman's mangled face, I realized we were all she had. We were her avenging angels, and she was worth it.

We are the ones willing to do the dirty work to protect the innocent.

CHAPTER 39

THE TRUTH HURTS:
PROTESTORS AND RIOTERS

I am excluding protestors who exercise their right to voice their opinion about an issue that is a valid one and do it peacefully. It is their right, but I still have yet to see a major protest or protests regarding the loss of our freedoms and the sellout legislation of our elected officials. In Europe, citizens took to the streets in protest of the TPP (Trans Pacific Partnership), but here in the U.S., the majority of citizens know nothing about it or the potential negative effects it will unleash on many aspects of American life and freedoms. This is because the average American is ignorant while he worships his television set and pays homage to his almighty sports team.

The protests we are used to seeing presently, however, are comprised of ignoramuses beyond belief, of all colors, including weak white fools who know nothing of what they are protesting for, and would never protest against what is really happening to their own race. Blacks themselves are either ignorant of the facts or too afraid to stand up for what is right in their own communities. Last but not least, thugs are only using protesting as an excuse to run wild violently and do what naturally comes to them.

Regarding police brutality, the ignorant public and those who deny the truth, protest issues and events they do not have all the facts for. If done peacefully, any protest will allow your voice to be heard and if valid, will get your message across and may make a positive difference. When protesting devolves into looting, smashing windows, stomping on vehicles, arson, pulling out innocent citizens into the streets for a beat down, and throwing missiles at cops, this is no longer protesting, but rioting and criminality. You no longer deserve the label as protester, but you now earned the name of Thug. This applies to black, white, and any other color or race who engages in the animalistic behavior that goes along with it. Presently we are being told that Thug is similar to the word nigger. That's ridiculous. The journalists, who are trying to push more political correctness and apologies onto the public, instead of being disturbed by what these criminals do, are themselves thugs and at the very least, punks.

The police have to put a stop to this type of behavior for the sake of the law and those who abide by it. Citizens do not deserve to have their property burned down while they are kept in fear as cops stand idly by and watch it all happen. Shameful. Ferguson, MO is a prime example of this, but there are many others, such as the recent Baltimore riots, etc. This seems to be a trend of all or nothing policing; overkill or impotence.

Protesters ostracize and protest against police who, during violent confrontations with violent criminals, defend themselves or others because of criminal actions. At least these protestors could pick their battles better. Backing the thugs that have sparked all these upheavals will not gain them any real sympathy, but will only add fuel to the fire and prove their stupidity. There are some legitimate arguments against police brutality. There are some valid reasons for a protest; however, it seems everyone who holds up a Black Lives Matter sign is judge, jury, and executioner on matters they either know nothing about or ignore completely, regardless of evidence. They are fueled by media lies meant to provoke hatred and fear. All credibility as protesters is lost when they loot and destroy property because they didn't get their way. It gives them the chance to act out in their own childish and uncivilized manner.

When these riots and protests are funded and recruited by the Jewish billionaire jack-off, George Soros with millions, it becomes an agenda that is truly a domestic terror threat to American public safety. Why is he not on the DHS terror list? I find no greater threat to America right now, on our soil, than someone who wants to incite riotous behavior and create racial instability on every street in America. He even has a billionaire bankroll to back it up with an insane ideology, but this is all common knowledge now for anyone who has looked into his background. For anyone who has not gotten off the couch and their hand out the chip bag, George Soros also funds Open Society Institute, Democracy Alliance, Moveon.org, Center for American Progress, Tides Foundation, Media Matters, etc., [cxxiii] and all of these are tied into his control of many areas within the mainstream media. This means the strong influence over the propaganda we are fed comes directly from his false ideology and funding. He also controls many politicians who espouse his far left agenda with campaign money.[cxxiv] You do not need a tin foil hat to see how dangerous a man like this is when he can actually pay looters and violent thugs to attend a protest and riot at any incident he decides to foment.

Black Lives Matter is a vile, racist, hate group that has been known to advocate for the killing of white people and police officers. They actually called for the lynching and hanging of innocent whites. They want to "turn the tide" and kill whites and cops to send a message about the "killing of black people in America."[cxxv] In addition, a Black Lives Matter affiliate radio broadcast had this to say:

> *"It's open season on killing whites and police officers and probably killing cops period. It's open season. Picking them off. Today we live in a time when the white man will be picked off."* He also said, *"It's about to go down, it's open season on killing white people and crackers."*[cxxvi]

This is beyond stupid! Blacks kill more blacks than anyone else, and they are their own worst enemies. Our society has done everything possible for these people, and it is never good enough. Now they want to kill us whites, and they can say it with impunity because there is no punishment or accountability for racial hatred unless it is committed by a white person. This is what happens when things are allowed to fester and become out of control, all under the watch of a black President and a black Attorney General. If someone who is white with a high ranking position criticizes the type of hate speech Black Lives Matter vomits out to the public, there is a higher potential for punishment.

For example, Surf City's Police Chief in North Carolina called Black Lives Matter a terrorist group, which they are, on his Facebook page. The Mayor called him to an emergency meeting regarding his post. The Chief retracted his post, apologized, and was still forced to retire from his position to avoid being fired.[cxxvii] This is incomprehensible. Politics as usual. Black terrorists can call for the genocide of white people and the blatant killing of police officers with no punishment whatsoever, but those who call them what they are (terrorists) receive the above treatment. This is a world turned upside-down.

According to the Center on Juvenile and Criminal Justice, police killings of blacks are down, 70% in the last 50 years. In 2012, 123 blacks were killed by police with a gun. In 2012, 326 whites were killed by police with a gun.[cxxviii] These are telling statistics, because blacks are responsible for the higher percentages of violent crime, and are actually being engaged less than whites by cops. In light of this information, I would like to dispel with these statistics, and not with hype or slogans, that black males are not an "endangered species" at the hands of police. This is simply a false ideology filled with propaganda used as fuel for a racist anti-white agenda.

CHAPTER 40

MANO EN MANO

Part of having muscles and the reputation I had is getting challenged by other cops who want to knock you down a peg. You have to take these challenges or you'll get ribbed for not doing it. Throughout my career I have been challenged by Captains, Sergeants and patrolmen, both veteran and rookie, all wanting their chance to take on Supercop. Here are just a few of them.

"Lancia! Get in here!" As I was walking by the patrol office to go to my locker, my shift Captain, a red headed Italian with a husky build and in good shape, called me in. "I'm ready for another go, Lancia." I had beaten this Captain at arm wrestling before, and my partner always loved watching these bouts and knew that the Captain would, as usual, take his defeat well. I asked my partner before going into his office, "Should I let him win this time?"

"Hell no, fuck him!"

When I walked in he was already sitting at his desk with his biceps bulging in his tight, short sleeved shirt. Back then a lot of us were in shape and we did not need to hide ourselves behind baggy uniforms. "Let's go Lancia, I'm gonna kick your ass this time."

"Okay boss. If I beat you again though, you're not gonna put us on a shit detail for punishment are you?"

"You're already assigned to the worst section of the city. What more can I do to you? If I win, you're going to have to buy me coffee, that's your punishment." He knew how to press my buttons. Arm to arm, I let him have one second of what he thought could be a victory before I wrenched his arm down as if he were an old woman across from me. He was really upset, so I tried to make him feel good about it.

"You did better that time, Cap."

"Damn it Lancia! Get the hell outta here- go back to your post!"

At one of the Union meetings, which we attended at times, I would always be accosted by a cop who was experiencing extra bravado that day. "Come on muscles, let's go!" This time it was a dapper Polish cop who was well liked by everyone including me. He was heavier than I was and taller, but I never let that stop me before. We affectionately called him, "The Polack." Arm to arm, I took him down easily. I made the mistake of saying, "Come on, you didn't even try this time." He had actually given it his all and was upset at me for saying that. He got over it pretty fast however, and challenged me on other occasions. Same results though.

After I had a few years on the job and had built up more of a reputation, even rookies wanted a shot at me. One Irish rookie, a six foot five, three- hundred pounder who dabbled in weightlifting, approached me one day after lineup and before we hit the streets. We had a nice crowd of half the platoon watching us.

"Hey Lance- right here, right now."

"You sure you wanna be humiliated with half your platoon watching, Rookie?"

"Jim- look at *me*, and look at *you*." He made his pectoral muscles move under his shirt. "I'm gonna make you cry," he said good naturedly.

"Just because you can make your tits dance doesn't mean you can beat me." I could not refuse him even though I actually thought this guy would give me some problems, as he outweighed me by a hundred pounds.

I took him down much faster than I thought I would. I wanted to teach him a lesson for what he said. He had a sore arm after that, because I took him down particularly hard and fast. While he was massaging his arm I told him, "You'll just have to jerk off with the other hand for a few days." He never challenged me again.

Young and strong. Me and my partner from Tactical Division enjoying a beer after work.

CHAPTER 41

BLEEDING OUT

When I was a teenager my friends and I would go to a pizza place on the East Side of town. Bridgeport had plenty of good pizza joints, but every once in a while we would like to go to this one. It was a fun place to hang out in and the owner, Tony from Brooklyn via Italy, didn't mind us making a little noise. His pizza was fantastic, but you had to endure Tony's insults which included a heavy use of the words "numb-nuts," "shit for brains," and "hey, moron!" Playful as they were, in today's sensitive society, he'd be out of business.

"Hey Tony, how ya doin? My partner and I will take two of your famous large pies."

"Eh, Jimmy, you still gotta da pimples, eh?" Same old Tony, to point this out in front of some pretty young female patrons should have been expected. "Yeah, still got a couple, I'm twenty-three years old and they should've been gone by now. Maybe it's your greasy pizza that does it."

In his famous, heavy Italian-Brooklyn accent Tony replied, "Nobody say you gotta eat it!"

"Red 42."
"42's on East Main.
"42-Proceed to Bridgeport Hospital. Use a code. Reports of a man with a gun."
"42. Copy that"

Tony's pizza would have to wait.

Once a thriving Polish neighborhood. Now it is uninhabitable.

We didn't say anything while speeding to the hospital with lights and sirens. You try not to think too much about the call so you can react. Nothing is as you expect usually, and it is impossible to plan for it.

"Red 42. We now have reports of shots fired in the hospital. Use caution."
"42 Roger that. Approaching the ER of Bridgeport Hospital now."
"10-4, 42. The time is thirteen-forty five."

Entering the doors of the emergency room, the nurses and doctors were in a frenzy. They pointed to the elevator and yelled, "Fourth floor, fourth floor!"

"Tell me what happened" I asked while we were on our way to the elevator wasting no time.

"Some guy shot his wife in her bed!" My partner took the elevator and I took the stairs to cover all bases, because as far as we knew he was still on scene. Our guns drawn, we both reached the fourth floor at the same time. It did not take much to know in which room the incident occurred, due to the bloody spatter on the open door. There were no doctors and nurses in sight, and it was eerily quiet. They were hiding. When we approached the room in question, a horrific sight unfolded. An unfortunate woman, who happened to be the shooter's wife, was in the hospital for injuries received by her husband earlier in the day. He had come back to finish his work. Blood was on the walls as if it had been thrown there. She was already dead, and had she bled out right there on her hospital bed. There would have been nothing doctors or nurses could have done for her. Now where was the shooter? He couldn't be far. We checked the bathroom and he wasn't in the small room, nor was he under the bed.

"Did anyone see where the guy went or what he looked like?"

A nurse from behind the counter spoke up in a timid, fearful voice. "He was Hispanic I think, wearing a tan jacket." She was still hiding and they were all terrified. Not everyone is built for this kind of thing and I understood that.

"Did you see where he went?" No, no one did. "You can come out now and attend to the woman."

My partner and I proceeded to check as much as we could on the fourth floor, and during our search for the suspect, we noticed footprints leading to the staircase which ended our search there. We followed the blood trail downstairs and the blood was diminishing to a point where we had to guess that he ran down to the first floor and to an exit there. One of the ER patients waiting to be attended to, along with doctors and nurses, was frantically pointing to the front entrance where we now had our first glimpse of the suspect.

We ran outside after him, and I saw a man in tan walking fast looking behind him. We bolted after him, and when he saw us he ran. We commanded, "Stop! Stop!" After a brief foot chase, we arrived at the location where I last spotted him, but he had disappeared. He could not have gone too far. A witness calmly pointed to a bush in front of a house. It was all we needed. We surrounded the bush, pointed our guns, and yelled. "Come out now, or we're gonna shoot!" No response. "I'm fuckin' shooting right now!"

From the bush came the man's voice. "Oh-kay, tek it easy-I come out!"

"Throw the gun out!"

"Oh-kay, Tek it easy."

"Stop telling me to take it easy you fucking asshole! Come out now and throw the gun out- let me see your hands!"

He tossed his bloody pistol from the bush and came out. He was a small man with a big gun. We tossed him to the ground and cuffed him, read him his Miranda rights, and then asked him, "Why did you kill your wife?"

He never said anything. He just smiled.

CHAPTER 42

"BEAT THAT WHITEY!"

Tensions between the races are nothing new. As a police officer in the areas I worked in, I would see the worst of it, and I had also grown up with it all of my life. It was difficult for me with all the hatred blacks had toward whites to sympathize with the overall, popular politically correct view of the supposed white racism against blacks-which is simply absurd in reality. I do not believe you should confuse racism with a white person's instincts of self preservation. Staying clear of blacks is not racism, but a survival tactic for many. I saw the real side of racism. In a public housing complex such as Father Panik for example, most everything the inhabitants had was provided for by the government through tax dollars; the rent, food, medical care, utilities, the heating, and the repairs to the damage they caused.[cxxix]

They destroyed their own neighborhoods.

I grew up in real poverty. Nothing was available for us, the working poor, by the government. Nor would we have taken it if it was offered. My mother, while pregnant with me, would walk miles to work to get to her factory job. When my dad's old Jalopy broke down, in order to get to work he would strap down his tools, which he carried in his handmade toolbox, onto an old lawnmower with the engine removed. This he pushed the two miles needed to get to his job site until his vehicle was repaired. It embarrassed me as a kid to watch him push his tools down the street, but as I grew older, I realized he did this in order to provide for his family without excuses, complaints or blaming anyone, and I respected him for it. We also did not have medical or dental care, and because we could not afford it, I never had doctor or dental checkups. There were many times we went hungry, wore worn-out and ill fitting hand-me-down clothing, and I had holes in the bottoms of my sneakers, even in winter, but it all made me the man I am today. The man who rejects the white privilege/white guilt narrative. Fuck that shit.

Born in Bridgeport, Connecticut of Italian Immigrants, the kind that worked,
obeyed the law, never complained, and earned their own way.

"Huh, 'Welcome to the Jungle,' that wasn't on there yesterday. I like the song, though. It's fitting, isn't it?"

"Oh, look at that one, 'White people stank,' that must be for you, Jim." Ha ha, very funny. We were patrolling FPV and admiring the new artwork on the sides of the buildings.

"Red 42."
"42's on, The Drive."
"42. Proceed to the vicinity of building 38. Reports of a large altercation in progress."
"42; Roger that."

During this period in time, the federal government had contracted workers to repair damage to many of the buildings in FPV; broken light bulbs in the hallways, smashed windows, updating heating systems, and general cleanup of urine and fecal matter in every hallway and stairwell. Some of the workers were black and some were white.

"42 on scene. Large crowd and disturbance. Will advise."
"10-4; 42. Time is thirteen hundred."

All we could see as we exited our police vehicle were flailing arms and kicks. Whoever was the recipient of these assaults was in some serious trouble. As my partner and I approached at the run, someone in the crowd spotted us and shouted "5-0," and all of the cowards immediately ran away. It did not take me long to realize they had been beating a white male to a pulp, for reasons we did not know at this point. My partner stayed with the injured man, but I gave chase to the "men" who had been responsible for the gang assault. "Piece of shit, I gotta get one of these fuckers!" I told myself as the chase continued through the alleyways. I always hated to see violent attacks on innocent people.

They had too much of a head start on me and got away this time (a rarity in a foot chase with me), blending in with the large crowd which was a daily presence in the Hole. I could not leave my partner by himself while he was protecting the injured man, because the people who lingered around him looked as though they could be a threat. I ran back to my partner who was hidden behind the crowd of almost twenty people surrounding him. "Move the fuck out of the way! Back off – I said back off!" I told them.

"What the fuck is wrong with you people?" I asked the crowd, who by now had backed off, realizing I was about to crack some heads. My partner was kneeling on the ground trying to render assistance to the injured man, and he was shielding him to protect him from further harm. I will never forget that image; it is one of the many things that go untold to the public. If we had not arrived and scattered this vicious crowd, I believe the man would have been beaten to death.

"What the fuck are you doing here? Are you buying drugs?" I asked the man on the ground because he was white.

"I'm working, I'm working sir!" the man said as he spit blood on the ground. "I'm with the XX company…" He took a breath, shaking. I felt bad about accusing him of buying drugs, but these were the only white faces you would see here other than the city police.

"Red 42, requesting a Medic; building 38."
"42; 10-4 Medic on the way. What do you have going on there?"
"42. One of the government contractors was severely assaulted by a large crowd."

We sat the injured man up. "I didn't do anything wrong. I was cleaning up the stairwell when this group of black guys told me to 'get the fuck outta here, white boy- this is the Village, you don't belong here.' That's the last thing I remember."

"Can you identify any of them?"

"No sir. They were all black, what else can I say? Can you just please get me out of here?"

CHAPTER 43

LONDON'S BOBBIES

On an unofficial visit to the U.S., two London law enforcement officers or "Bobbies" were requesting ride-alongs to observe American policing. Their first stop, of course, was New York City, then some New Jersey shithole that I can't remember, maybe Newark, and lastly Bridgeport, because of its reputation and because it was less than an hour's drive from the New York City limits. The three cities chosen were within the Tri-State Metropolitan- New York Area. Our Lieutenant called my partner and me off the street at the beginning of our shift and told us we were to take these two London police officers on a ride-along within the limits of our post, but only for an hour or two unofficially and as a gesture of international professional courtesy. Our post happened to be the worst area in the city and our Lieutenant wanted to show them a good time.

Our guests hopped in the backseat, and looking around said, "You Americans and these bloody cages." This was in reference to the metal cage separating the prisoners from the officers in the front seats.

We laughed and told them things were different here. It happened to be summer and typically busy. They were aware of the statistics after researching and told us, "Supposedly Bridgeport has a crime rate that exceeds that of New York City and other major cities in the U.S."

"Yeah, that's true." My partner was a man of few words. So I spoke up.

"That's why you're here, right?" I asked him.

The bearded Londoner told me, "Yes, correct." After the awkward start, things were even quieter in the car. Must have been the "language barrier." After learning our names, the smooth faced Bobby piped up. "My word, there are so many Italian police officers in this area."

"Yeah and Irish mostly."

"Yes. Irish." Judging by the tone of his response I guessed he didn't like the Irish. Do the English get along with anybody?

"You New Yorkers have the most difficult accents to understand."

"You're the ones with the accents." My partner told them. As we were driving them through some of the more deplorable neighborhoods, I asked them, "So you guys don't carry guns?"

"Some do. Special units."

"What do you do when someone starts shooting, do you ask politely for the bad guy with the gun to wait for you to call a special unit?" My partner laughed, but these guys didn't think it was funny.

"America is still the Wild West. London has its crime, but very few gun related incidents occur," boasted one of the men in the backseat.

Shortly after this last awkward conversation, Dispatch called.

"Red 42. Respond to shots fired in the vicinity of the Hole, Father Panik Village. Possible two victims on the ground. Do you copy?

"Red 42 copy that. On the way. Is a medic responding?"

"Medic on the way. Any other cars in the area available to assist?"
"Red 41 will assist. On the way."
"Red 42 use a code."
"10-4."

When dispatch tells you to use a code that means lights and sirens. Lights and sirens on, the Londoners loved it and perked up considerably, just like two kids. A short ride brought us to the scene of the shooting in the worst part of the worst housing project in the United States. There were approximately 100 black males milling around, but there were no victims visible. I opened my door, but before exiting my vehicle, I turned to the Bobbies. "If you're gonna get out, you've got to do what we say."

"We'll stay here in the car and observe, Yank." He said this with a smile. I turned to my partner.

"Do you see anybody on the ground anywhere?"

"No, just shell casings. Nothing unusual." I asked the crowd if they had seen anyone get hit. Stupid question; all I received in response was laughing and asinine sound effects. Several buildings away we could hear more shots being fired. POP POP POP...POP POP. My partner said, "Sounds like a MAC-10." After a search and fruitless questioning, we realized there were no victims, at least not at this location.

"Red 42 on. Disregard the medic for now, and you can call Red 41 off. There are no visible shooting victims."
"10-4, thank you 42. Can you please respond to shots fired on Waterview Avenue?"
"Roger that-will do."

We headed back to our police car, which was now surrounded by black faces interested in the occupants of the backseat. This was something we were used to, but the Bobbies looked intimidated. "We heard shots, did you hear them? Sounded like machine gunfire."

"Yeah, we're gonna go check that out now. This is normal. When we respond to calls, they fire shots to try to intimidate us. They think they can keep us out of here and- hey, get the fuck out of my way assholes!" The Bobbies were amazed. Not only because of the amount of people menacing about, but at the way they had parted for me like a sea of black. They asked us, "Will you be calling your special unit or SWAT team?"

"For what, the shots fired?" We laughed. "What SWAT team? We *are* the SWAT team- we handle all this shit ourselves." On approaching the vicinity of the shooting, we exited the vehicle and our London brothers asked us if it was wise to go out. "We have to, it's our job. Do you want to come?"

"Certainly!" They came out feeling and looking like police officers, encouraged by our casual response. One even found the shell casings from the MAC-10 and gave them to us for evidence. I told him "thanks, but it won't do any good unless there's a victim here."

"My God, these guns are on your streets like it's a warzone!"

"Yeah, even bigger ones that that one. And it is a warzone." Shots fired were a daily occurrence, but the shooters were long gone. Our guests were amazed at the bleakness of Father Panik, and knew themselves from the FBI statistics of its notorious ranking. They were finally glad to be here and riding with us, and we were starting to like them even though they *were* British.

"For Yanks and Italians, you're pretty good fellows. Will you oblige us and take us back to the station now?"

"Seen enough?"

"Yes, we've seen what we came here for and have other matters to attend. You men handled yourselves brilliantly. If you ever come across the Pond, look us up. Here's our cards. We'll take you around and show you some real policing, London style."

Victim of urban blight. A neighborhood too close to Father Panik Village.

CHAPTER 44

ALWAYS EXPECT THE UNEXPECTED

Puerto Rican is better than Italian food? Are you out of your fucking mind? I've never had a girl beg me to take her to a Puerto Rican restaurant! I mean, you only can take rice and beans and fried bananas so far!" My partner for the day was a replacement for my regular partner, and he was a proud Hispanic trying to convince me that the food of his native land was superior to all others, including Italian. Funny thing about this conversation is that we were on a break eating Chinese food at the time. We both had a good laugh over our cultural differences.

"Red 42."

"Damn!" I threw my plastic fork down and started the car. "Once this shit gets cold it's no good."

"42's on."
"42. Reports of a Hispanic male threatening a crowd with a weapon. Two thousand block of William Street."
"42, what kind of a weapon?"
"42. Uh, caller states a gun."
"10-4, on the way."

"Nice of him to tell us it was a gun." I told my partner as we packed up our Chinese food for later consumption.

"42's on scene. Large crowd here."

As we exited our police vehicle several frantic people in the crowd yelled, "He's got a gun, he's got a gun!" and were pointing to the suspect who was now fleeing at our arrival and running towards an alley. We immediately gave chase and followed him there. As the foot chase continued, the suspect turned in a crouched position and attempted to fire his weapon at us. My gun was already drawn and so I fired a shot at him in our defense, and so did my partner who fired twice. Our shots deterred him from following through with his threatening move. We continued on foot and caught up to him near the crowd in front of some row houses. "Freeze! Don't move!" I yelled, and the suspect stopped and threw his hands up in the air, but they came down quickly. He was acting in a strange manner, and as we approached and cuffed him, I brought him to the ground and noticed blood on his shoulder. Other cops were now on scene. "Call for a medic, we hit him."

Apparently, when he turned to shoot, one of our bullets hit the mark, but the wound was not serious enough to stop him so he was able to continue running while we were unaware that he had been shot. The ammunition issued at the time was the 125 grain semi jacketed hollow point bullet. The reason police departments use hollow point ammunition is because if lethal force is necessary, the hollow point round is least likely to go through the suspect and cause further damage to anyone else, especially in an urban setting. But in this case, the suspect was fortunate enough that when the bullet entered him it struck his clavicle, which turned the bullet and allowed it to exit without mushrooming. I frisked him and found no weapon on him at this time. We learned at a later time that he had the opportunity to hand his gun to his girlfriend before we caught up to him, he collapsed, and was handcuffed. Seeing he was shot and in pain, I uncuffed him to relieve some of his discomfort. I asked one of the other officers on the scene, "Is a medic on the way?"

"Roger that. Medic is on the way." This all happened ten minutes after we were happily eating Chinese food and enjoying some laughter. Thankfully, the wound was not fatal and the suspect fully recovered. This is the nature of police work; normal one minute and chaos shortly after. The reasons for this disturbance and threats by the suspect were unknown to us at the time, and until the situation is under control, all we could do was react to the crowd's fear of an armed man and how he decided to react towards us. The "what" and "why" always comes later in the following investigation.

CHAPTER 45

THE TRUTH HURTS: HOLLYWOOD AND TELEVISION

Movies, television shows, commercials, Disney, MTV, and others are just a part of the myriad of trash that spews out racial biases against whites, anti-Christian messages that are now being bludgeoned over everyone's head, and the corrupting effect of commercialized pop culture propaganda. Not to mention the glorification and normalization of alcohol and drug use. This has all been done so progressively, it has become normal. It is a well known fact that generally, television and Hollywood are owned and run by Jewish elites.[cxxx] I have never seen any defamation of any religion other than Christianity and any other race other than the non-Jewish white race. I find this highly offensive myself, because I am a straight, strong Christian white male- the main target for these progressive assholes and their attacks. This defamation is directly linked to much of the violence against whites and has created a perpetually tense racial atmosphere, fomenting this violence and at times even falsely validating it. If a Christian owned media network bashed Jews in any way, it would be called anti-Semitic and would be shut down. Is there a term for being anti-Christian that instills that kind of fear and public backlash? No. If you are in Hollywood and complain about this you will be blacklisted and publically ostracized as a bigot for exposing bigotry. Amazing. Why does anyone's religion or race need to be singled out in this culture that falsely preaches equality and diversity? It is a communist style control on all the entertainment garbage that enters our homes and feeds the minds of the masses.

So called "celebrities" get away with the most asinine and condescending statements, all within and in homage to what is accepted as either political correctness or popular opinions beyond what is right. Some of the more recent and offensive racist, anti-white and hateful language comes from talentless ass-bag Jaime Foxx who, on Saturday Night Live while promoting his stupid racist movie, told the audience, "I get to kill all the white people, how black is that?" The audience consisting mostly of pathetic whites applauded him like the weak, fearful, morons they are.[cxxxi] Jaime Foxx forgets that without the white majority he would not be who he is today, whatever that is. Oprah Winfrey, a billionaire made in part by the admiration of the white majority, says those same whites need to "die" so racism can end,[cxxxii] because she suddenly decided that white people were the problem. If an old, fat, rich, black woman, who has everything, can have these sentiments and get away with it, what can we expect from the rest of the racist anti-white black population? She escapes accountability and never apologizes, and Paula Deen suffers publicly for making a joke decades ago. There is no fairness here, and the ones claiming they are treated unfairly are not only deluded, but get a free pass on betraying the liberal left's and their own twisted ideals of racial equality.

These are just two examples of the incredible stupidity and mentality of people who could make a positive difference in society but fail to do so in order to placate the destructive gangster thug mentality, which only manifests their fear of them. These types of statements and attitudes lead to, perpetuate, and provoke the lawlessness we are experiencing today. These people ignore the masses of young black teenagers looting, destroying, killing, raping, robbing, and engaging in racially motivated mob attacks across the country, all while shouting "It's a black world,"

"Fuck whitey," "Kill that Cracker," etc. All this happens while the public is told that it is impossible for blacks to be racists. What a crock of shit.

This is our future. These are not old white people perpetuating racial hostilities who need to die off so it can all end; this is just beginning for the next generation. How is a white America supposed to feel when these blatant, anti-white and hateful racial insults go on with impunity? This is another side effect of Critical Race Theory being taught in public schools to children and teens. Any parent who allows this to be taught in their tax funded schools, is complicit. Concerned parents need to fight back and have it removed from their school's curriculum.

Another blatant misrepresentation of facts that Jewish controlled Hollywood and our media generates is the misconception that all serial killers are either white males or females. Wrong again, very wrong in fact. According to statistics dating back to 1900, black serial killers not only existed but have actually been the majority of serial killers since 1990 to 2010.[cxxxiii] The media and Hollywood persist in racially profiling white males to represent the lunatics that are serial killers when it is a factual lie.

The music industry is no different; gangster rappers, calling themselves "artists" are applauded and celebrated on mainstream television, movies, and media for targeting the young as recipients of their racist, anti-white, misogynistic, and violent lyrics which are all destructive to malleable minds of all races. Can any of this be good for not only the young to hear, but for anyone? This only emboldens them to continue their rampages and to become worse than they are. Look at the trend of black thuggery and the emulation of it by all races and cultures, most notably whites, who in their moronic attempts to mimic the gangster mentality prove just how impressionable the public is. It would be laughable if it were not so destructive to our culture and society.

CHAPTER 46

THE TRUTH HURTS: THE UGLY FACE BEHIND THE HATE AND WHITE GENOCIDE

When you look at Jewish power in the United States, you will see that for the less than 2% of their population here they have a preponderance of control. For instance, they have complete control of Hollywood as stated previously, the media, newspapers, magazines, publishing companies, the internet, music and porn industries, and international banking systems. Jews own and run the U.S. Federal Reserve, and run and control Wall Street. Jews comprise 50% of U.S. billionaires and are over-represented as Supreme Court Justices (four out of nine are Jewish), and in our legal system in general. They control our education system which includes public schools and state colleges and universities, our medical system, control of our military, Congress through lobbying, the White House through their overrepresentation in our government to their population percentage, head the CIA, hold high ranking foreign and domestic policy positions in our government, run our Homeland Security, head our FDA, and many more elements of American society are Jewish Zionist controlled and driven.[cxxxiv] These Talmudic Zionist Jews all have dual citizenship with the United States and Israel and admit that Israel is where their allegiance lay. They are actively trying to silence all dissent and criticism of their dominance in our society, as well as in Europe and elsewhere.

The United States, through taxpayer dollars, gives billions in aid to Israel, while falsely lauding them as our "best ally" in the Middle East. When has "our best ally" used any troops or treasure to aid us in fighting our "mutual enemies" in any war? Many top Jewish officials are openly derogatory to anything American and their hatred for Christians and whites is not only reflected in their Talmud, but in many of their actions as well as their speech. I regard it as hate speech by their own definition. The ADL should apply their own parameters of offensive speech to police themselves and stop being such massive and manipulating hypocrites.

These are just a few of the outrageous, hateful statements from their own lips:

"If we get caught they will just replace us with persons of the same cloth. So it doesn't matter what you do, America is a Golden Calf and we will suck it dry, chop it up, and sell it off piece by piece until there is nothing left but the world's biggest welfare state that we will create and control. Why? Because it's god's will and America is big enough to take the hit so we can do it again, again and again. This is what we do to countries that we hate. We destroy them very slowly and make them suffer for refusing to be our slaves."- **Transcribed quote taken from an audio recording of Netanyahu at a meeting at Fink's Bar, Jerusalem, 1990.** [cxxxv]

"I want to tell you something very clear: Don't worry about American pressure on Israel. We, the Jewish people, control America, and the Americans know it." –**Ariel Sharon, October 3, 2001.**[cxxxvi]

It is in the Jewish interest, it is in humanity's interest that whites experience a genocide. Until white children are burned alive, white women raped, mutilated, murdered, and all white men who have not been slaughtered watch

133

powerlessly as their people are terrorized: only then will mankind be on a more equal footing, ready to discuss white privilege and the apparent chip on the shoulder that minorities have." – **Rabbi Ishmael Levitts**[cxxxvii]

If these quotes do not shock you, this one should do it:

"Gentlemen. Welcome to the Second Centennial Meeting of the Learned of Elders of Zion. We have achieved all of the objectives expressed at our first meeting 100 years ago. We control governments. We have created dissension among our enemies and made them kill each other. We have effectively silenced criticism of our affairs and we are the richest race of men on this earth.

Many of you are very busy men. Let us get to the crux of the matter. As masters of business, politics, law and most importantly… media, we are ready to implement our most important and ambitious program. One that will finally and totally remove from existence the impediments of our absolute control of this earth.

I speak OF THE DEATH OF THE WHITE RACE. The complete removal of all means of reproduction of the so-called Aryan race. Men, we now control the destiny of this race. It is now time to make sure the White race becomes extinct through miscegenation and having a virtually zero birth rate.

We have all enjoyed the vision repeated all over this world every day of THE LAST WHITE CHILDREN playing with little dark children and knowing that they are being set-up for their eventual destruction. We can ruin THE ANCIENT PURE BLOODLINE OF AN ARYAN CHILD by convincing him or her of the altruism of begetting interracial children. We must expose the race mixing of the urban centres to the suburbs and rural areas of this country.

More aggressive programs to integrate these areas are now underway through HUD. It is worth any price to annihilate the next generation of White children. We want every White father to feel the sting of having their children marry colored mates and produce biracial children. We must use our power to discourage White men and women who still persist in getting together from producing more pure White children.

They will be ostracized by not becoming part of the New Society of all races. This will dissuade most of them. We will deal with the less cooperative goyim by murder and imprisonment.

Finally, we will SEE THE END OF THIS WHITE RACE. Impressionable White children will have their minds moulded into the agents of their own destruction.

Already, our efforts have succeeded in making the "men" of this race grovel at our feet. Men, you and your ancestors have worked hard to make sure we would have the power to hold the destiny of this race in our hands. Now we have it. Perish Aryan Goyim (cattle)!" [Applause] End of speech. - **'The National Observer' via a document from Abe Foxman's [Jew A.D.L. president of USA] office. August 25, 1998, New York, NY.**[cxxxviii]

These quotes are genocidal hate speech spewed out by the Jewish ADL and members of the Israeli government and clergy, our "greatest ally." This is no longer something to be ignored. They have achieved their goal in Europe through the massive Islamic and African "refugee" migration, which they are very open and vocal about,[cxxxix] all funded by Jewish Zionists through the European Union. George Soros tops the list of funders for the genocide of the European white race, bringing with it crimes of murder, rape, assault, theft, loss of European culture, and all the miseries associated with these. As their foot soldiers, they use already hate filled people, blacks Hispanics, and Muslims, with anti-white and anti-Christian ideologies and false religions such as radical Islam. Sharia Law is not too far from becoming implemented in these countries that were once Christian nations. Still think white genocide is a ridiculous notion?

I discus the Jewish connection in this book because all the relating factors have much to do with the declining quality of life in the U.S., morally, racially, financially, culturally, and criminally. So yes, this topic has a place here in my book because we need to know who is behind much of our society's moral decay and why. The results of this deliberate manipulation of our way of life directly leads to crime, violence and despair on our streets. This affects all of us because you, the public, get the shit end of the stick and all that comes with it, while police have to clean up and deal with the mess that all this deception and evil leaves behind. We see this happening in Europe even now where self defense in most cases, is met with arrest and monetary fines while Jewish funded hordes of Africans and Muslims rape, assault, murder, and pillage at will against the native white European with impunity. Many European police departments are being told to stand down and allow these crimes to be committed, and for certain areas to be called "no go zones" for police to patrol. This emboldens the criminal element and creates a nightmare of racially fueled chaos. The fallout from forced racial integration and immigration, wars fought for the benefits of Zionists, impoverishing whites through affirmative action and lower hiring standards for minorities, and ignoring a true white genocide happening in South Africa, has all contributed to the decline of the worldwide European white demographic which has plummeted from 25% of the global population in 1950, to less than 8% today. This happened while all other non-white races have been enabled to exponentially grow in number. You need to think on that for a while.

We need to stop being afraid to talk about this Jewish Zionist influence in our society before this violence and hate becomes a normal and accepted way of life. We need to expose this issue, hold those behind it accountable for their hate speech and actions, and be unafraid to confront it.

"I know the blasphemy of them which say they are Jews, and are not, but are the synagogue of Satan"
–Revelation 2: 9, King James Version

CHAPTER 47

GANGLAND

The 1970's and 80's was an extra violent period of activity for the "mafia." There were many notable mob figures that were publicly "wacked" during struggles for position, power, and general housecleaning. Because Bridgeport was under the control of the five crime families of New York, there were many mob related incidents that happened there and in surrounding towns during those years. One of these involved Frank Piccolo, who was a Captain in the Gambino Crime Family of New York. He had been sent to help a "friend" of the "family," who just happened to be none other than Wayne Newton, when the superstar planned to purchase the Aladdin Hotel and Casino in Las Vegas.

Newton was close to Piccolo's cousin, Guido "The Bull" Penosi, who offered him a favor whenever it was needed. Newton took him up on that offer, when both he and his daughter were threatened after a business deal fell through. Penosi sent Piccolo, who lived in Bridgeport to Vegas to handle the situation. Before he left, Piccolo sat down with members of the "family" for permission to act. The family, without the need for Piccolo, took matters into their own hands and ended the threats. After this, threats against Newton's friend, Mark Moreno, began and the singer contacted Piccolo directly. Piccolo again requested a meeting and sat down with members of the Family where they agreed to help, and again the threats stopped.

Piccolo then decided that because he had helped the super wealthy singer twice, that he was entitled to earn a little something extra. He began to blackmail Wayne Newton and his friend and fellow entertainer, Lola Falana. Both Piccolo and Penosi stood trial for attempted extortion of Newton, and while Penosi was acquitted, Piccolo's case was moved to a higher court. On September 19, 1981, before Piccolo was able to stand trial, he was gunned down, gangland style, in a phone booth near his home in Bridgeport.[cxl]

* * *

"Priority- All available vehicles in the area of Main and Jewett. We have reports of automatic weapons fire. At least one victim down in a phone booth."

Patrolling the east side that day and miles away, none of the Red Sector cars could respond to this call. As it was, there was more than enough police coverage. Not too long after police arrived on scene, they had a suspect vehicle and description of the shooters. A van carrying three white males opened fire on a mob figure who was making a call in a phone booth. In other words, this was a true mob hit. The victim in this case was Frank Piccolo.

A short time after this information was made available to us, the Stratford police reported visually identifying the suspect vehicle and surveilled it into a Stratford home. Stratford is a neighboring town adjacent to Bridgeport and where some mafia types would reside. Stratford PD was a small department, and unable to handle what everyone expected would result while trying to apprehend the shooters armed with AR-15s.

Red Sector.

"All Red Sector Units report to patrol office immediately. Use a code."

"41. I'm on this Signal 20 you sent me to." One of the other red sector cars called in and was handling an accident at the time.

"41. Disregard that. I'll get another unit to take care of that."

"42, 43, and 40. Do you copy? Report to the patrol office immediately."

"42, 10-4. On the way"

"40, roger that."

"41. 10-4."

I arrived at the patrol office and all shift supervisors were present there with the Boss, and some detectives were there as well. The captain greeted us with my favorite words. "Let's get into the arsenal and get some firepower." He briefed us on what our assignments were and we all grabbed shotguns, extra rounds, and flack vests.

"Hey, Cap, what about those Thompson .45's, can I take one of those?" In our arsenal there was a beautiful group of about twenty .45 caliber Thompson machine guns that dated from the 30's and 40's. I don't know if they were ever used, but they were impressive.

"Just take the fucking shotgun, Lancia; I don't want you to hurt yourself." We armed ourselves quickly. There were eight patrol officers from Bridgeport's Red Sector; these were picked because we worked in this high crime dangerous area. If anybody was going to handle this, it would be us. At this time our Tactical Unit was not active, there was no SWAT, and as I said before, the street cops handled everything. I was elated and so were the men with me. We did not know what was going to happen, but we were ready and we knew the guys we were going after were not shy about shooting. After all, they gunned down a mafia Capo in broad daylight in a phone booth. That's pretty bold, but we were bold too.

We took the short drive to Stratford and met up with their PD as soon as our lights and sirens could get us there. The house was surrounded and we were ready with shotguns loaded. As we approached the house to take up positions and ready ourselves for the firefight we knew was coming, we were approached by a Stratford PD Sergeant. He informed our Lieutenant that the suspects had slipped away before they could cordon off all the escape routes. Although we had arrived at the scene quickly, Stratford's small department did not have enough officers to cut off their escape.

Anti climatic, yes, that's exactly how I felt too. They got away and eluded Stratford PD. It took us a while to calm down after being prepared to engage in a gunfight of the magnitude we were expecting. After we searched the area in our patrol cars, we were ordered back to Red Sector, but to be ready for another call back if the suspects were sighted. The call never came.

Sometime after Piccolo's funeral, where mourners such as Frank Sinatra were in attendance, the assailants were apprehended, tried and sentenced.

CHAPTER 48

THE TRUTH HURTS: SO CALLED BLACK LEADERS AND POLITICIANS

Racists, money grubbers, opportunists, perpetuators of violence. These race-pimping fools have actually set civil rights advancements into a retrograde, but instead of being shamed for this, they are celebrated by the public and the media as they ram their racist agendas against whites into everybody's face. They ignore the fact that the worst problems in black communities are their own young black males and females acting out in a most uncivilized, irresponsible, ungrateful, and sometimes inhuman manner. Al Sharpton, the court jester of civil rights (who is also a regular guest at the White House), Jesse Jackson, and Louis Farrakhan are the most outspoken, and are the worst of the worst. These charlatans masquerade as "civil rights advocates" but represent all of the above. There are others, but collectively recent events only showcase their impotence and refusal in making any real grounds regarding improving the lot of their people or social race relations.

I can write an entire book on Al Sharpton and his racist antics, but everyone knows enough about him. Same with Jesse Jackson, although he does admit there is a problem in the black community that has nothing to do with whites. He even went so far as to say, "There is nothing more painful to me at this stage in my life than to walk down the street and hear footsteps... then turn around and see somebody white and feel relieved."[cxli] After all his "efforts" for the black community, he is still afraid of his own people, and he is not alone. But why is it perceived as racist when a white person feels threatened by black thugs with their pants hanging down to their ankles, when it is completely justified to be apprehensive about a demographic that is statistically known to be more violent?

Louis Farrakhan has been inciting a race war by calling for 10,000 volunteers to kill whites. He said to his audience in a Baptist Church in August of 2015:

"I'm looking for 10,000 in the midst of a million. Ten thousand fearless men who say death is sweeter than continued life under tyranny. Death is sweeter than continuing to live and bury our children while the white folks give our killers hamburgers. Death is sweeter than watching us slaughter each other to the joy of a 400-year-old enemy. Death is sweeter. The Quran teaches persecution is worse than slaughter. Then it says retaliation is prescribed in matters of the slain. Retaliation is a prescription from God to calm the breasts of those whose children have been slain. So if the federal government won't intercede in our affairs, then we must rise up and kill those who kill us; stalk them and kill them and let them feel the pain of death that we are feeling!"[cxlii]

These ignorant, overtly anti-white terror threats were spewed out in front of an applauding crowd of black "church-goers." If this does not send up a red flag to normal Americans, I do not know what would. Is Farrakhan on a DHS domestic terror watch list? This church was filled with thugs as far as I am concerned. To Louis Farrakhan I say this: you are a thug, and if you were going to go after the people responsible for killing your own, you would have to start with the black thug community who kills more blacks than any other race out there. Blacks are their own worst enemies, but are always looking for someone else to blame.

The black man's worst enemy is the black man and his violent thuggery.

When you condone, excuse, and blame others for failure on an epic scale, the problem only worsens and everyone suffers. But then again, if these leaders actually did something constructive, such as help these youths to choose a difference path and learn personal accountability, they would be out of a job and out of the limelight. Even Martin Luther King Jr., who I believe was a race agitator and profiteer, is quoted as saying in Saint Louis in 1961:

"Do you know that Negroes are 10 percent of the population of St. Louis and are responsible for 58% of its crimes? We've got to face that. And we've got to do something about our moral standards.....We know that there are many things wrong in the white world, but there are many things wrong in the black world, too. We can't keep on blaming the white man. There are things we must do for ourselves."

How many major cities that are completely run by black Mayors and minority staffs, backed by millions of federal funding, are completely in the decline and collapse? Why are jobs of any type not provided for the citizens of their cities and for, most notably, young black males and females? Everyone complains about no opportunities for blacks, but when blacks are in the positions to provide these jobs, they fail to do so. You cannot blame that on "white privilege."

Black Mayors throughout recent history have all failed in trying to set an example. When blacks have control of their own destiny and people, they fail to thrive and make their communities better. They polarize and terrorize the whites that are left, and then white flight is the result. Can you blame them? They also call this "flight" a form of racism, because whites do not allow themselves to be terrorized or victimized by staying put.

The cities that are now run by blacks in political power are now hollow shells of what they once were. These are facts and I wish it could be different, but so do most Americans. In most recent news the black female Mayor of Baltimore, Stephanie Rawlings-Blake, has made a fiasco out of the recent rioting over the arrest and death of Freddie Gray. Regardless of the root causes of the issue, the Mayor allowed protests to devolve into riots, looting, and attacks on white citizens and business owners. She is quoted as saying, "We gave those who wished to destroy, space to do that as well," and enacted the curfew for the city a full two days after the beginning of the rioting. Why not immediately? She also had her officers stand down during the looting, and told them to back off and retreat when the crowd became out of hand and when they threw missiles at them.[cxliii] She allowed thugs to destroy homes and businesses, beat white citizens, rob, and commit larceny throughout the city and disrupt its normal functions.[cxliv] So it comes down to this, she is either incompetent and unable to handle being the Mayor of a large city, or she is doing what she is told to do by someone higher up, which makes her a puppet.

Black Baltimore Prosecutor, Marilyn Mosby, used the media to try and convict the six officers in Freddie Gray's death, only 24 hours after she skimmed the files on the case. Instead of addressing the public in a way that made us confident there would be a trial without bias or prejudice, and instead of promising true justice in a court of law with a jury of one's peers, Mosby used the time to bloviate her statement on national television and to push her perception of social injustice. *"To the people of Baltimore and the demonstrators across America. I heard your call for 'no justice, no peace.' Your peace is sincerely needed as I work to deliver justice on behalf of this young man…To the youth of this city, I will seek justice on your behalf. This is a moment. This is your moment…You're at the forefront of this cause, and as young people, our time is now."*[cxlv] This is not how a prosecutor speaks to the public about a case she should, by all ethical standards, have recused herself from due to multiple conflicts of interest. Speaking to the public about an impending case is not the time to talk about social and racial causes, or to discriminate against other members of the public based on age and race. Her statements are not only inciting and provoke racial hatred, but are unprofessional and leave little room for confidence in our judicial system.

The family of thug Freddie Gray was awarded $6.4 million by the city of Baltimore. Just one more example of glorifying thugs.

I cannot think of one major city that has benefited from having a black president, a black attorney general, or a black mayor. It seems it is a recipe for disaster when more money than ever before, via our tax dollars, is pumped into these cities and the same results are manifest. These cities systematically get worse and worse, and the minority community continues to complain without end. It is interesting to note that under "President" Obama, black unemployment is at an all time high.[cxlvi]

Similarly and internationally speaking, we need only to consider the plight of South Africa. Putting aside all the rhetoric about the "evils" of Apartheid which only separated races, the bottom line is this: that under the white Apartheid rule, from 1948 to 1989 the whole of South Africa averaged 170 murders per year. This is surprisingly low for such a large country. When Apartheid ended and the former terrorist, Nelson Mandela became the country's first black ruler and for the years afterwards, it has averaged at least 25,000 homicides per year since 1994. This is after cooking their books and doctoring up the numbers because they are so outrageously high; the highest in the world in fact. They are also ranked the highest in the world for reported statistics of rape in that country. Many murders and rapes go undocumented, so the experts say the numbers may very well be twice that. Either way, it is the murder and rape capitol of the world. What could have changed so drastically since the end of "evil" Apartheid? Very few blacks in South Africa are happy with the situation as it is today, expecting more from black rule; many there say nothing has changed for the better, but for the worse.

The plight of the white South African is another story. They are systematically being discriminated against openly by the government and by the black people, and as high as the murder rate is there, whites are four times more likely to be murdered by blacks.[cxlvii] The most disturbing fact is that more than 85,000 racially motivated murders of white South Africans by blacks have been committed since the end of Apartheid in a deliberate agenda to eradicate everything white. These murders include torture, rape, dismemberment, burning the victim alive and ritualistic murders. The victims of these atrocities include men, women, children and infants, all of the white race. Without worldwide condemnation, the current president of South Africa, Jacob Zuma has openly and brazenly called for the killing of whites.[cxlviii]

Again there is nothing in the cowardly media whatsoever for these true victims, and most Americans are oblivious to what is happening over there. So the example here is that the world saw the "evil" system of Apartheid as oppressive and racist, but now with a black racist and openly anti-white government in complete control, we can easily see there is no improvement and in fact, it has devolved into the most violent country in the world. Who is to blame now? Not one mention in mainstream American media is made of this horrific situation. The worst part is, that the white South African cannot attain refugee status and are refused entry into their European countries of origin while hordes of foreign, non-white soldier aged males from the Middle east and blacks from Africa have the red carpet rolled out before them and all our treasure at their disposal as they are given refugee status for no reason at all.

Here in the United States there are a few black leaders who actually place the blame of the criminal actions of blacks, on blacks themselves. They are to be applauded, but are not. They are ostracized and threatened with death by the black community, their own people. They are ridiculed with such names as "Uncle Toms," "sellouts," "race traitors," and "wanting to be white," just for telling the truth and endeavoring to steer their communities into a positive direction. The mainstream media give these good black leaders very little coverage, and their credibility and motivation is always questioned. It is very unfair, especially to the black community who needs men such as these. If allowed to, these men can change the face of the black community for the positive. These commendable leaders include individuals such as Rev. Jesse Lee Peterson, Allen West, Sherriff David A. Clarke, and Ben Carson, just to name a few.

CHAPTER 49

SHOOTOUT AT THE OLD TRAIN STATION

During my career with the BPD I have made countless misdemeanor and felony arrests of murderers, rapists, shooters, drug dealers, armed robbers, muggers, perpetrators of assaults of all degrees, car thieves, etc. There were times when my partner and I would average seven felony arrests per work week, and this was in a regular patrol car. When I was in the Anti-Crime Unit, Tactical Unit, and Uniforms Division of Special Services, that number of felonies would be higher most of the time. We kept busy. Adrenaline plays a major role in the outcome of many dangerous encounters. I can tell you, however, that whenever any suspect is no longer a danger and surrenders, we were professional enough to know that force was no longer necessary. In the many situations I have been in where my gun could have been used, I used restraint always, and I have never seen a trigger happy cop in my time as a police officer. It was, is, and always should be the last resort.

"All vehicles in the downtown area standby... We have reports of State Police in pursuit of armed robbery suspects in a blue Toyota north on 95 proceeding towards Bridgeport."

"Any vehicle in the downtown area be prepared to assist State Police with the pursuit in case they get off a Bridgeport exit."

"Attention: State Police now reports suspect vehicle is getting off Exit 27 into Bridgeport. Render assistance."

"Red 42's on the way."

"22's not far."

"Amber 21 near the 95 exit into Downtown."

[Jumble on radio.]

"All vehicles stay off the air until you have engaged in the pursuit and have suspect vehicle in sight."

As we approached the downtown area I observed the State Police chasing the suspect vehicle and was able to join the chase right behind the state cruisers. Other BPD cars were engaging now, with lights and sirens everywhere.

"Red 42 in pursuit of a blue Toyota. State police is behind them. We are on Water Street in the vicinity of the Old Railroad Station"

"10-4, 42."

All the vehicles involved in the chase were all focused on the suspect car, which contained two masked armed suspects. In police jargon, we had a true "daisy chain" in progress. The car was chased into the parking lot of the old railroad station where the suspects felt they could elude us, but unbeknownst to them, the lot had no outlets or vehicle exits. After taking a circuitous route through the large open area and eluding the State Police, whose vehicles had spun out wildly on a turn due to the high speeds, my police vehicle was now directly behind them.

Realizing they could go no further, the suspects brought their car to a screeching halt. I stopped mine directly behind them at approximately 20 feet away from theirs. We got out and stood behind the doors, and while we were doing this, I noticed movement in the vehicle and then a shotgun was visible. All during this time other police cars were taking up position trying to surround the suspects. It was clear they were getting ready to shoot it out with us, as they had already fired shots at the scene of the robbery. When one of the suspects in the vehicle raised his weapon and pointed it at us, I unloaded several shots into their rear window, shattering it. One of the suspects stayed in the vehicle, probably hit by my gunfire. The other suspect ran with the shotgun until shots rang out from at least 10 other officers on scene who, in my estimation, fired approximately 50 shots. They all missed, including mine, as I also fired at the fleeing armed suspect. Anyone who has been in a firefight, whether it is in a war on foreign soil or on an American street combating crime, understands that missing a moving target is a common occurrence. The suspect wisely dropped his weapon at this point and sprinted towards the railroad tracks in a frenzy to get away from us. I was the only officer who gave chase on foot while the other cops approached the armed suspect who remained in the vehicle.

I chased the runner onto the old railroad tracks, which spanned as a bridge over the river, and told him to get on his knees or my next shot would hit the mark. He quickly went to his knees with his hands behind his head. He apparently was not a stranger to this position. I apprehended him, cuffed him, searched him for more weapons and then walked him back.

The State Police had a K9 unit involved in the chase, but the dog was too afraid to go over the railroad tracks because it feared the water 25 feet below. That seemed pretty funny to me when it was all over. My partner and the other officers on the scene had secured the driver, and after bringing the suspect back, we transported them to the station. We let the State Police have the arrest since they initiated the chase. Sure, let them do the paperwork. I remember they said that Bridgeport cops were "cowboys" for the amount of shots fired, but they were glad we were there to apprehend these violent suspects for them.

"You guys need to do some more firearms training. Out of all those shots, someone should've been hit!" We all laughed.

I was surprised I didn't hit the runner or the driver, but I noticed one of my shots did hit the intended target. The driver was a black male with a huge natural or afro, and I noticed two bullet grazes that burned nice tracks into his hairdo. Both suspects were so shaken after the shootout and the chase, they were relieved to be arrested and not killed or even wounded after having so many shots fired at them. One of them said to the State Police officer, "Take me out of Bridgeport, I'd rather be in jail."

I believe cops in general are not trigger happy and would prefer not to use their weapons, but of course there are the occasional "bad apples." A good cop is never afraid to engage in a firefight, because this is a very real possibility every time he puts on his uniform and patrols his beat. If you are afraid of this, you really have to find another profession or find a desk job. I believe the best cops, when facing danger, use this as a last resort. I have never witnessed a fellow police officer wantonly fire his or her weapon in an unjustified manner.

CHAPTER 50

THE TRUTH HURTS: GUN CONTROL ADVOCATES

There are two ways to look at these morons. First, if they really think that crime can be stopped or cut drastically by taking legal guns away from honest American gun owners, they are living in a dream world. Every city with the highest crime statistics has the strictest gun control laws in the country. This means the criminals still and always will have weapons obtained illegally and will kill and shoot with impunity, without fear of a possible victim being armed or able to protect themselves.

For example, on average, 87% of causes of death in Chicago are due to gun violence, which increased 50% last year even with stricter gun control laws.[cxlix] I am using Chicago as the poster child for gun control to expose the ignorance of gun control advocates while showing the futility of further infringement on our Second Amendment Rights. In the first month of 2016, Chicago experienced a record high in gun violence with 51 homicides and more than 241 shooting incidents.[cl] These shocking statistics are not a result of law abiding gun owners acting irresponsibly; they are members of black gangs running rampant and unchecked with illegal guns.

Across the board, major cities with strict gun control laws are the highest statistically in gun violence. In fact, since 2009, 92% of America's mass shootings have occurred in *gun free zones!* [cli] Interestingly, gun violence overall peaked in the 1980's to the early 90's and as police officers we faced it head on at the street level and we went to war with it. Since that time, gun violence is down 50% across the nation.[clii] Unfortunately, according to a poll, 56% of Americans actually believe gun violence has gone up,[cliii] which is a direct result of a lying, agenda-driven mainstream media and a government rhetorical campaign hell-bent on legal gun confiscation. This is disturbing, because the government knows very well that overall gun violence is down, strict gun laws do not work, and criminals will always get guns, especially if they are brought across the border as fallout from Fast and Furious, courtesy of the United States government.

In case you know nothing about history, here is a little lesson. What do these infamous dictators have in common: Mao Tse Tung, Joseph Stalin, Pol Pot, and Idi Amin? These all disarmed the masses before taking total control while executing and killing millions of their own people. Our government is well aware of this. They are also aware of the reason we have a Second Amendment, and it is disturbing to me that with millions upon millions of our taxpayer dollars, the government funds Islamic militants, trains them and arms them in the pretext of overthrowing tyrannical governments in the Middle East so they can gain "freedom." We also cannot forget Fast and Furious where our government armed drug cartels in Mexico, again with our tax dollars. All this is done while our own government is actively planning to disarm every law abiding American gun owner, especially with recent executive orders bypassing Congress. This is all looming under the United Nation's "UNODA" which stands for, "United Nations Office for Disarmament Affairs" which directly points to lawful American gun owners as a target for disarmament in its overall goal of global disarmament. [cliv] Our government is working furiously and illegally to accomplish this. Former Attorney General Eric Holder adamantly stated in 1995, "We need to do this every day of the week and just really brainwash people into thinking about guns in a vastly different way."

Recently, in Britain, citizens were required by law to turn in all handguns and consequently, gun violence rose 35% in the same year, and criminal use of handguns rose 46%.[clv] Similarly in Australia, guns were ordered turned in and gun violence rose immediately.

One would have to be a complete and utter fool to believe that taking guns away from legal owners would reduce crime and gun violence. The criminals will still have them, and they do not care how many laws are enacted to restrict gun ownership. Get this through your thick skulls.

The real culprit in fueling every one of these horrific mass shootings in the past 20 years is the shooter's use of psychotropic drugs, legally prescribed by doctors who are fully aware of the side effects that directly lead to this type of violent behavior.[clvi] However, President Obama received 20 million dollars in campaign funding by pharmaceutical companies and the health care industry,[clvii] which helped to prop him up on his throne. This is why you will not hear the President condemn these prescription drugs as the root cause of this type of gun violence. We must all remember that our elected officials are bought and paid for by lobbyists who can put this kind of money out.

The other way to look at gun control supporters is as hypocritical liars who know the facts but still want to take away guns from law abiding citizens as their only means of protection, and leave them exposed to the growing armed and violent criminal element. Again, every tyrant in history has disarmed their people before taking total control over their lives and committing atrocities upon them.

Divide the people, disarm the people, conquer the people.

Bridgeport police investigate at Washington Auto Supply, Barnum Avenue, the site of an attempted robbery and shooting Thursday.
Telegram photo by Wayne Ratzenberger
THE TELEGRAM, Bridgeport, Friday, August 5, 1983 Metro

Man shot, but foils robbery

My partner and I at the scene of another shooting. Gun violence was much higher in the 1980's than it is today.

CHAPTER 51

THE PRIEST

Even the most benevolent, caring, and well meaning people have a breaking point, and it says something about those who would push these types of individuals past their natural limits.

"Red 42"
"42's on. building 44 on that stolen car. It's just getting hooked up now."
"42. When you're done with that, head over to the Catholic Church on the corner of Hallet and Church Street. Priest reports a break-in."
"Red 42, 10-4. As soon as we're done here."

"How many times has this church been broken into?" I asked my partner, who shrugged his shoulders in answer. This particular church had been built in the late 1930's for the new Yellow Mill Village, later to be called the Father Panik Housing Project; the first of its kind in the state of Connecticut. This church would have been fully attended by the factory workers and their families who lived in the Village, back then a nice place to live. But those days were long gone.

"There he is- he looks pissed!"

"42's on scene."
"10-4 42."

"Good afternoon, Reverend. How can we be of service?"

The Priest was outside the church when we pulled up, pacing back and forth with a broom in his hands. "This is the third time this month alone! They steal everything- I hear them at night!" We went inside the church, which was a modest size building and had been a beautiful place of worship that was once fenestrated with stained glass. These had long since been broken and repaired with plexi-glass windows.

"What did they do this time, Sir?"

"They desecrated the alter and stole the chalices. I replaced them so many times, and they did it again! The candleholders are gone." He looked around in despair and pointed. "They urinated over there. There's nothing left to take." As I was writing down the stolen items for my report, he sat on one of the benches and cried out. "This project was built for the poor! To give them a decent community to live in!" He shook his head. "Over the years it has turned into the hell that it is now. I reach my hands out to them all the time. Our charities bring clothes and toys for their children. There are some good people here still, but fewer every day." He paused while I was writing my report. I wanted to give him some breathing space, so I did not ask him anything further. I felt he may have just needed a sympathetic shoulder at this point. All of a sudden he looked up from the floor and cried out.

"These fucking niggers! I don't know what to do! I was here for them, and I can do nothing anymore, nothing! I've got to get out of here. Forgive me," he said, ashamed, as he put his face in his hands and cried briefly. After a few seconds he regained his composure.

"It's alright, Reverend, we all have those days." I put my hand on his shoulder, but then removed it realizing there was absolutely nothing I could do or say to change anything. "Do you have any idea who did this?" He looked at me but did not answer. "We patrol the church as much as we can. We'll try to come by more often and maybe write our reports parked outside. If you hear anyone inside, day or night, call us. Maybe we can catch them in the act." Knowing the futility of this, he stood up and nodded, unable to speak. He did not look us in the eye. After glancing around at the damaged church, he shook his head, walked into the back room and shut the door.

CHAPTER 52

END OF AN ERA

Becoming a cop at eighteen was a great opportunity for me. I went in and came out of the academy with high hopes and wanting to be fair and judicious. I thought I could change just a little of the world around me. All this sounds cliché and naïve, but wouldn't the world be a better place if we all thought this way? I found that after time and experience, I could merely plug up some of the wounds in a bleeding society. Sometimes those wounds reopened and sometimes they hemorrhaged. Just being there kept a bandage on a festering sore just waiting to burst. Society changed significantly during my tour, from the old way to the new, from peace keeping and justice to appeasement. Who was being appeased? It was certainly not those who were law abiding and peaceful. This appeasement reaches new heights even today where thugs, such as Ferguson's Michael Brown, are glorified to the point a memorial is installed in the very place he broke the law, terrorized the owner of a business, and robbed his store before resisting a police officer's efforts to make him accountable.[clvii] Talk about glorifying thugs.

As a street cop I have seen just about everything humans are capable of, every form of bad, inhumanity, evil, and very little good. I have saved lives, taken dangerous criminals off the streets, put fear into dangerous men to keep them from becoming more dangerous, and my presence made people feel safe. I patrolled dangerous streets at night while people slept and my presence there was like a lion among ravenous hyenas, and I kept them in check. I worked in elite units, with many different police agencies, and did more to keep crime at bay than most cops ever will. I am proud of who I am and of my service to the people of the city I lived and worked in.

After seeing all the terrible things most people never experience unless they are victims, it weighs heavy, and it wears a cop out after time. I truly believe that when the job starts to jade you to a point where you cannot perform your duties with enthusiasm any longer, you have to leave. It is not the type of profession that you can do "half-assed," because people will suffer for it. Before I left the police force, I was contacted regarding my promotion to acting detective, which would lead to a permanent position as a police detective. I declined, knowing my time was past, even though the position, after time, would have increased the amount of my pension. The will to holster my gun and pin the badge on my chest no longer gave me the same pride or passion. It was my decision and my decision alone to end my career when I did. Working the most dangerous post in the United States in constant high gear was enough. Even my last arrest was made while I was off duty, assisting other officers to apprehend a murder-rape suspect that was terrorizing the city. I had given Bridgeport all I had.

Whatever good I did I am proud of, but today's society looks on an Alpha Cop as a rogue, and has demonized him mercilessly, when instead he should be a reminder that crime can be kept under control without soldier cops on the street treating all, for the sake of "equality," like criminals and the enemy. Although we are all equal under the law, we are not all equal; law abiding citizens are not thugs or criminals. When you engage police violently and partake in criminality, you take a risk and have to deal with the consequences. Likewise cops must know that they are there to protect the public and never to treat them all like the enemy. The public must know that each cop is an individual, and not all are the same. They are not all good, but they are not all bad either. I fear that regardless of what is right or wrong, regardless of what would be best for the safety of all the citizens of this country, and because of the direction we are heading in, the Alpha Cop will be persistently demonized until he is non-existent, thugs will continue to be glorified, and the police will eventually become militarized and federalized. Both will oppress you more than ever before. Once this happens, there is no going back.

Notes

The Choice to Live or Die

i. Valerie Richardson. "Cops Kill More Whites than Blacks, But Minority Deaths Generate More Outrage." *The Washington Times*, April 21, 2015 http://www.washingtontimes.com/news/2015/apr/21/police-kill-more-whites-than-blacks-but-minority-d/?page=all

ii. Klein. "Beyond a Simple Solution for Ferguson." *Time*, Aug 21, 2014. http://time.com/3153340/beyond-a-simple-solution-for-ferguson/

iii. Mike Males. "Who Are Police Killing?" *Center on Juvenile and Criminal Justice*, Aug 26, 2014. http://www.cjcj.org/news/8113

iv. Dirk Johnson. "In Bridgeport A Sharp Rise in Murder Rate." *New York Times*, Jan 26, 1987. *http://www.nytimes.com/1987/01/26/nyregion/in-bridgepoprt-a-sharp-rise-in-murder-rate.html?pagewanted=1*

Eighteen

v. McCarthy, Peggy. "Father Panic Village: High Hopes Are Now Despair." *The New York Times*, Aug 2, 1987. http://www.nytimes.com/1987/08/02/nyregion/father-panik-village-high-hopes-are-now-despair-l-by-peggy-mccarthy.html?pagewanted=1

Built For War

vi. CBS DFW. "FBI: 80 Percent of Police Officers are Overweight." 14 Aug. 2014. http://dfw.cbslocal.com/2014/08/14/fbi-80-percent-of-police-officers-are-overweight/

The Truth Hurts: The Media

vii. Tucker, Eric. "A Federal Pilot Program Aimed at Reducing Racial Bias May be coming to Your City." *Huffington Post*, Mar 12, 2013. http://www.huffingtonpost.com/2015/03/12/six-cities-racial-bias-pilot-program_n_6859160.html

viii. Hudson, John. "U.S. Repeals Propaganda Ban-Spreads Government Made News to Americans." *Fox News Nation*, Jul 15, 2013. http://nation.foxnews.com/2013/07/15/us-repeals-propaganda-ban-spreads-government-made-news-americans

ix. Flaherty, Colin. *White Girl Bleed A lot*. Washington, D.C.: WND Books. 2013.

x. Brian Rogers. "Mystery of Boy's Death Remains as Capital Murder Trial Looms." *Huston Chronicle*, Aug 9, 2013.

xi. Mommot, Michael, "15 Years Later Tawana Brawley Has Paid 1 Percent of Penalty." *NPR*, Aug 5, 2013. http://www.npr.org/sections/thetwo-way/2013/08/05/209194252/15-years-later-tawana-brawley-has-paid-1-percent-of-penalty

xii. Salomon, Evie. "60 Minutes Investigates: The Duke Rape Case." *CBS News*, Apr 12, 2015. http://www.cbsnews.com/news/60-minutes-investigates-the-duke-rape-case/

xiii. Ibid.

xiv. David McCormack. "Hunt for Thugs Who Attacked Commuter on St. Louis Train after He Refused to Answer Question about Michael Brown's Death." *Daily Mail*, 29 Mar. 2015. http://www.dailymail.co.uk/news/article-3017271/The-shocking-moment-commuter-assaulted-St-Louis-train-refusing-answer-charged-question-Michael-Brown-s-death-no-one-steps-help.html

xv. Devega, Chancey. "Charleston Church Massacre: The Violence White America Must Answer For." *Salon*, 18 Jun, 2015.http://www.salon.com/2015/06/18/charleston_church_massacre_the_violence_white_america_must_answer_for/

xvi. Watson, Paul Joseph. "Charleston Shooting: Liberals Call For Disarming All White People." *Infowars*, Jun 18, 2015. http://www.infowars.com/charleston-shooting-liberals-call-for-disarming-all-white-people/

xvii. Block, Dustin. "10 Shot, One Fatally, At Child's Birthday Party in Detroit." *MLive*, Jun 21, 2015. http://www.mlive.com/news/detroit/index.ssf/2015/06/9_shot_on_detroit_basketball_c.html

xviii. CBS Philly. "17 People Wounded, Including 6 Kids, In 2 Shootings in Philadelphia." Jun 23, 2015. http://philadelphia.cbslocal.com/2015/06/23/17-people-wounded-including-6-kids-in-2-shootings-in-philadelphia/

The "P" Word

xix. Flaherty, Colin. "Heisman Hopes Hit By Black Mob Attack. Wave of Violence Lands Hard on Campuses." *WND* Oct. 16 2012. http://mobile.wnd.com/2012/10/heisman-hopes-hit-by-black-mob-attack/

xx. Noble, S. "Latest Outrage: DOJ Will Only Prosecute White on Black Hate Crimes." *Independent Sentinel*, Dec. 28 2013. http://www.independentsentinel.com/latest-outrage-doj-will-only-prosecute-white-on-black-hate-crimes/

xxi. Violence Against Whites. "Statistics." https://violenceagainstwhites.wordpress.com/statistics/

The Truth Hurts: Political Correctness

xxii. Wing, Nick. "Ayo Kamathi, Racist Homeland Security Employee, Says 'War is On' After Being Put on Leave." *Huffington Post*, Aug. 26 2013. http://www.huffingtonpost.com/2013/08/26/ayo-kimathi-racist_n_3818883.html

xxiii. Wing, Nick. "Ayo Kamathi, Homeland Security Employee, Has Side Gig Promoting Race War, Bashing Gays." *Huffington Post*, Aug 22 2013. http://www.huffingtonpost.com/2013/08/22/ayo-kimathi_n_3794900.html

xxiv. Ross, Chuck. "Valdosta State Student Who Stomped US Flag Wants to Kill All White People." *The Daily Caller*, May 23, 2015. http://dailycaller.com/2015/05/23/valdosta-state-student-who-stomped-us-flag-wants-to-kill-all-white-people/

xxv. McClelland, Mac. "The New York Times Rape Friendly Reporting." *Mother Jones*, Mar 9, 2011. http://www.motherjones.com/rights-stuff/2011/03/new-york-times-texas-rape

xxvi. "NBPP Leader Sued for Defamation." *Council of Conservative Citizens. http://conservative-headlines.com/2015/01/nbpp-leader-sued-for-defamation/*

xxvii. Council of Conservative Citizens. "Up to 28 Black Males Participated in Gang Rape of 11 Year Old." *Conservative Headlines*, Mar 12, 2011. http://conservative-headlines.com/2011/03/police-up-to-28-black-males-participated-in-gange-rape-of-11-year-old/

xxviii. Encyclopedia of Murderers. "Mona Yvette Nelson." *Murderpedia, http://murderpedia.org/female.N/n/nelson-mona.htm*

The Hole

xxix. Stowell, Linda, "Father Panik Village Still Plagued by Crime, Money Problems," *Associated Press*, Apr 2, 1988. http://www.apnewsarchive.com/1988/Father-Panik-Village-Still-Plagued-By-Crime-Money-Problems/id-d3a64f1081322347f791ea177f3187e8

xxx. Ibid.

xxxi. "To Stop Drug Sales, Bridgeport Barricades its Streets," *The New York Times*, May 18, 1993. http://www.nytimes.com/1993/05/18/nyregion/to-stop-drug-sales-bridgeport-barricades-its-streets.html

xxxii. Rearden, P. & Jerry Thornton. "Going Private Doesn't Help Life in Project," *Chicago Tribune*, Jul 06, 1987. http://articles.chicagotribune.com/1987-07-06/news/8702190204_1_public-housing-residents-federal-housing-officials-private-management

xxxiii. Capiello, Janet. "Once Bustling Connecticut City Struggles with Leper Image," *Deseret News*, Jun. 16, 1991. http://www.deseretnews.com/article/167789/ONCE-BUSTLING-CONNECTICUT-CITY-STRUGGLES-WITH-LEPER-IMAGE.html?pg=all

xxxiv. Lavoie, Denise. "Father Panik Village Now a Criminal's Paradise: Bridgeport Conn Complex is being Vacated and Demolished as Officials Give up in Face of Drugs, Decay, and Death. *Los Angeles Times*, Jan. 09, 1994. http://articles.latimes.com/1994-01-09/news/mn-10073_1_father-panik

xxxv.   Johnson, Dirk. "In Bridgeport A Sharp Rise in Murder Rate." *The New York Times*, Jan 26, 1987, http://www.nytimes.com/1987/01/26/nyregion/in-bridgepoprt-a-sharp-rise-in-murder-rate.html?pagewanted=1

xxxvi.   Bridgeport Guardians Inc. TNT v. Delmonte AFSCME 15 1159 AFL CIO AFSCME 15 CIO USA. http://caselaw.findlaw.com/us-2nd-circuit/1475408.html

The "Do Nothings"
xxxvii.   Johnson, Dirk. "In Bridgeport A Sharp Rise in Murder Rate." *The New York Times*, Jan 26, 1987, http://www.nytimes.com/1987/01/26/nyregion/in-bridgepoprt-a-sharp-rise-in-murder-rate.html?pagewanted=1

The Truth Hurts: Black Males
xxxviii.   "Michael Nutter, Mayor of Philadelphia Church Speech, Sunday August 7, 2011." *YouTube, https://www.youtube.com/watch?v=vL0QFZBLca4*

The Truth Hurts: The New Jim Crow
xxxix.   Halyard, Helen and Mazelis, Fred. "A Brief For Radical Politics: The New Jim Crow by Michele Alexander. *World Socialist Website*, 18 Sep. 2012. https://www.wsws.org/en/articles/2012/09/crow-s18.html

xl.   Riley, Jason L. "The State Against Blacks: The Welfare State Has Done to Blacks What Slavery Couldn't Do…And That is to Destroy the Black Family." *The Wall Street Journal*, Jan 22, 2011. http://www.wsj.com/articles/SB10001424052748704881304576094221050061598

xli.   Ibid.

xlii.   National Institute of Corrections. "West Virginia: Overview of Correctional System. 2013 Crime." *NIC* 2014. http://nicic.gov/statestats/?st=WV

xliii.   Noble, Andrea. "Violent Crime in D.C. Surges in 2012." *The Washington Times*, Feb 19, 2012. http://www.washingtontimes.com/news/2012/feb/19/violent-crime-dc-surges-2012/?page=all

xliv.   Thorn, Victor. "Crime Stats Alarm Black Leaders." *American Free Press*, Jan 6, 2014. http://americanfreepress.net/?p=14864

xlv.   Forman, James Jr. "Racial Critiques of Mass Incarceration: Beyond the New Jim Crow." *Faculty Scholarship Series. Paper 3599.* 2012. http://digitalcommons.law.yale.edu/fss_papers/3599

xlvi.   U.S. Department of Justice. "Fact Sheet: Drug Related Crime." Sept 1994. http://www.bjs.gov/content/pub/pdf/DRRC.PDF

xlvii. NCADD. "Alcohol, Drugs, and Crime." *National Council on Alcoholism and Drug Dependence*. https://ncadd.org/for-youth/drugs-and-crime/230-alcohol-drugs-and-crime

xlviii. NAACP. "Death Row, USA Winter 2015." 2015. http://www.naacpldf.org/files/publications/DRUSA_Winter_2015.pdf

WTF? 911 For Cops?

xlix. Wing, Nick. "27 Police Officers Were Slain in the Line of Duty in 2013, The Fewest in More Than 50 Years." *The Huffington Post*, Nov 24, 2014. http://www.huffingtonpost.com/2014/11/24/police-officers-killed-2013_n_6213940.html

l. Balko, Radley. "New ACLU Report Takes A Snapshot of Police Militarization in the United States." *The Washington Post*, Jun. 24, 2014. http://www.washingtonpost.com/news/the-watch/wp/2014/06/24/new-aclu-report-takes-a-snapshot-of-police-militarization-in-the-united-states/

li. Lind, Darra. "Cops do 20,000 No Knock Raids A Year. Civilians Often Pay the Price When Things Go Wrong." *Vox*, May 15, 2015. http://www.vox.com/2014/10/29/7083371/swat-no-knock-raids-police-killed-civilians-dangerous-work-drugs

lii. "Family of Woman Killed in a Botched Drug Raid to Receive 4.9 Million." *CNN*, Aug. 16, 2010. http://www.cnn.com/2010/CRIME/08/16/georgia.botched.raid/

liii. Barnett, Ron and Alongi, Paul. "Critics Knock No Know Police Raids." *USA Today*, Feb 13, 2011. http://usatoday30.usatoday.com/news/nation/2011-02-14-noknock14_ST_N.htm

We Were the Good Guys

liv. Thompson, Paul. "Parents of Murdered British Students Criticise Barack Obama." *The Telegraph*, 29 Mar 2012. http://www.telegraph.co.uk/news/worldnews/northamerica/usa/9173820/Parents-of-murdered-British-students-criticise-Barack-Obama.html

lv. "Remembering Chris and Shannon." 2007. http://www.chrisandchannon.com/

lvi. Auster, Lawrence. "The Truth of Interracial Rape in the United States." *Front Page Magazine*. May 3, 2007. http://archive.frontpagemag.com/readArticle.aspx?ARTID=26368

The Truth Hurts: Federal Government Agencies

lvii. Hamner, Suzanne, "Obama Looks to Unconstitutionally Takeover Local and State Police," *Freedom Outpost*, Mar 3, 2015. http://freedomoutpost.com/2015/03/obama-looks-to-unconstitutionally-takeover-local-and-state-police/

lviii.   Tarlowe, Stu. "When the Government Targets Constitutionalists." *American Thinker*, Feb 13, 2014. http://www.americanthinker.com/articles/2014/02/when_the_government_targets_constitutionalists.html

lix.   Gerstein, Josh. "Eric Holder: Black Panther Case Focus Demeans 'my people.'" *Politico*, Mar 1, 2011. http://www.politico.com/blogs/joshgerstein/0311/Eric_Holder_Black_Panther_case_focus_demeans_my_people.html

lx.   Noble, S. "Latest Outrage: DOJ Will Only Prosecute White on Black Hate Crimes." *Independent Sentinel*, Dec 28, 2013. http://www.independentsentinel.com/latest-outrage-doj-will-only-prosecute-white-on-black-hate-crimes/

lxi.   The Conservative Treehouse. "No More Hesitation" – Homeland Security and Police Dept. Request Targets For Shooting Practice To Help Desensitize Law Enforcement To Shooting Average Americans…" Feb 20, 2013. http://theconservativetreehouse.com/2013/02/20/no-more-hesitation-homeland-security-and-police-dept-request-targets-for-shooting-practice-to-help-desensitize-law-enforcement-to-shooting-average-americans/

lxii.   Mc Nelly Torres and Willard Shepard. "Family Outrage After North Miami Beach Police Use Mug Shots as Shooting Targets." *6 South Florida, Jan 17, 2015*. http://www.nbcmiami.com/news/local/Family-Outraged-After-North-Miami-Beach-Police-Use-Criminal-Photos-as-Shooting-Targets-288739131.html

lxiii.   Siegler, Kirk. "Year After Denying Federal Control, Bundy Still Runs His Bit of Nevada." *NPR*, Apr. 14, 2015. http://www.npr.org/2015/04/14/399397139/year-after-denying-federal-control-bundy-still-runs-his-bit-of-nevada

lxiv.   Judicial Watch. "Obama Asserts Fast and Furious Executive Privilege Claim for Holder's Wife," Oct 23, 2014. http://www.judicialwatch.org/blog/2014/10/obama-asserts-fast-furious-executive-privilege-claim-holders-wife-2/

lxv.   Lanier, Candice. "U.S. Government: Evangelicals, Catholics, & Ultra Orthodox Jews Are Serious Threats to National Security." *Mario Murillo Ministries*, Apr 15, 2013. https://mariomurilloministries.wordpress.com/2013/04/15/federal-government-lists-evangelical-christianity-as-a-top-terrorist-threat/

lxvi.   "Kill The Crackers, Kill Them All." *YouTube*, https://www.youtube.com/watch?v=DDb2byj74oY

lxvii.   Bosca, Brooke. "Thug Tells Whites: Bow Down To Blacks, You're all Gonna Die!" (Video). *Top Right News*, May 20, 2015. http://toprightnews.com/thug-tells-whites-bow-down-to-blacks-youre-all-gonna-die-video/

lxviii.   Snyder, Michael. "Illegal Immigration Nightmare: Obama Has Been Releasing 1000s of Convicted Criminals Back Into Our Communities. *Infowars*. Jun 20, 2015. http://www.infowars.com/illegal-immigration-nightmare-obama-has-been-releasing-1000s-of-convicted-criminals-back-into-our-communities/

lxix.   Sacchetti, Maria. "ICE's Sex Offender Policy Under Scrutiny: Globe Investigation Finds Many Violent Sex Offenders Released but Not Closely Tracked or Forced to Register." *The Boston Globe*, Jun 14, 2015. https://www.bostonglobe.com/metro/2015/06/13/ice-freed-sex-offenders-often-without-notifying-states/v14qAOXKUOqAtaFeKGeGWI/story.html

lxx.   Snyder, Michael. "Illegal Immigration Nightmare: Obama Has Been Releasing 1000s of Convicted Criminals Back Into Our Communities. *Infowars*. Jun 20, 2015. http://www.infowars.com/illegal-immigration-nightmare-obama-has-been-releasing-1000s-of-convicted-criminals-back-into-our-communities/

lxxi.   Gibson, Dave. "Illegal Aliens Committed 500 Child Sexual Assaults in North Carolina During January." *Before Its News*, Feb 22, 2015. http://beforeitsnews.com/politics/2015/02/illegal-aliens-committed-500-child-sexual-assaults-in-north-carolina-during-january-2691762.html

lxxii.   Ibid.

lxxiii.   Tani, Maxwell. "The Chilling Murder of a San Francisco Woman Has Roiled the Immigration Debate." *Business Insider*, Jul. 11, 2015. http://www.businessinsider.com/kathryn-steinle-murder-immigration-sanctuary-cities-2015-7

lxxiv.   http://www.history.com/this-day-in-history/castro-announces-mariel-boatlift

lxxv.   See "The Truth Hurts: The School Systems."

lxxvi.   United Nations Treaty Series. "Convention on the Prevention and Punishment of the Crime of Genocide," 1948. https://treaties.un.org/doc/Publication/UNTS/Volume%2078/volume-78-I-1021-English.pdf

lxxvii.   Dykes, Aaron. "James Woolsey Denies CIA Media Control." *Infowars*, Mar 3, 2011. http://www.infowars.com/james-woolsey-denies-cia-media-control/

lxxviii.   "CIA Admits Using News To Manipulate The USA." *YouTube, https://www.youtube.com/watch?v=ds-PhWsXqOg*

lxxix.   Ibid.

lxxx.   N.C.O.I.C. "John Stockwell: The Secret Wars of the CIA." http://ncoic.com/ciawars.htm

lxxxi.   Loewenstein, Antony. "The Ultimate Goal of the NSA is Total Population Control." *The Guardian*, 10 Jul, 2014. http://www.theguardian.com/commentisfree/2014/jul/11/the-ultimate-goal-of-the-nsa-is-total-population-control

James Lancia

J.A.W.S.

lxxxii. Riedel, Charlie. "US Police get Antiterror training in Israel on privately funded trips. Reveal. Sep. 16, 2014. https://www.revealnews.org/article-legacy/us-police-get-antiterror-training-in-israel-on-privately-funded-trips/

lxxxiii. "Black Teens Beat A White Motorist to Death With A Hammer in St. Louis." *Council of Conservative Citizens*, Nov. 30, 2014. http://conservative-headlines.com/2014/11/black-teens-beat-white-motorist-to-death-with-a-hammer-in-st-louis/

lxxxiv. Kelly, William. "Police Chief Blames 'Pilgrims', Cops for Chicago Violence." *Fox News Nation*, Jun 27, 2012. http://nation.foxnews.com/chicago-violence/2012/06/27/police-chief-blames-pilgrims-cops-chicago-violence

lxxxv. Ross, Chuck. "'Glad That He Is White' Kentucky Sherriff Says of Suspect Shot by Deputies. [Video]" Daily *Caller*, May 13, 2015. http://dailycaller.com/2015/05/13/glad-that-he-is-white-kentucky-sheriff-says-of-suspect-shot-by-deputies-video/

lxxxvi. Diliberto, Gioia. "In Bridgeportscam, the FBI Gets Caught With its Pants Down-Literally." *People*, Sep 7, 1981: 16.10. http://www.people.com/people/archive/article/0,,20080148,00.html

lxxxvii. Madden, Richard. "New Page in Bridgeport's Police Story." *The New York Times*, Jul 29, 1984. http://www.nytimes.com/1984/07/29/weekinreview/new-page-in-bridgeport-s-police-story.html

The Truth Hurts: Militarized Police

lxxxviii. Geller, Pamela. "Obama Administration and UN Announce Global Police Force to Fight 'Extremism' in US. *Brietbart*, Oct 2015. http://www.breitbart.com/big-government/2015/10/02/obama-administration-and-un-announce-global-police-force-to-fight-extremism-in-u-s/

lxxxix. Commission on Accreditation for Law Enforcement Agencies, Inc. *"Tier One Standards. Standards for Law Enforcement Agencies: A Management Improvement Model Through Accreditation. 5th ed."* July 2006, Revised 03/24/2014-APD. P. 18, Article 1.1.2.

xc. Maag, Christopher. "Police Shooting of Mother and Infant Exposes a City's Racial Tension." *The New York Times*, Jan 30, 2008. http://www.nytimes.com/2008/01/30/us/30lima.html?_r=0

xci. Daily Mail. "Government Killed One of Their Own: Iraq War Vet and Father of Two Shot 71 Times in Own Home by SWAT Team." http://www.dailymail.co.uk/news/article-1389437/Iraq-war-vet-marine-Jose-Guerena-shot-71-times-Tucson-home-SWAT-team.html

xcii. Krause, Joshua. "Cops Who Flash-Banged Infant's Crib Are Blaming the Baby." *The Daily Sheeple*, May 21, 2015. http://www.infowars.com/cops-who-flash-banged-infants-crib-are-blaming-the-baby/

xciii.   Dykes, Melissa. "U.S. Court Ruled You Can Be 'Too Smart' To Be A Cop." *Global Research*, Dec.18, 2014. http://www.globalresearch.ca/us-court-ruled-you-can-be-too-smart-to-be-a-cop/5420630

Damsel in Distress

xciv.   "Victims Final Moments Caught on Store Surveillance." Dec. 28, 2011. http://www.wistv.com/story/16407832/victims-final-minutes-caught-on-store-surveillance

xcv.   Johnson, Dirk. "In Bridgeport A Sharp Rise in Murder Rate." *The New York Times*, Jan 26, 1987. http://www.nytimes.com/1987/01/26/nyregion/in-bridgepoprt-a-sharp-rise-in-murder-rate.html?pagewanted=1

Other Police "Duties"

xcvi.   Watson, Steve. "Elderly Couple Honk at off Duty Cop; Cop Breaks Man's Nose, Smashes Teeth Out With Gun." *Infowars*, May 13, 2015. http://www.infowars.com/elderly-couple-honk-at-off-duty-cop-cop-breaks-mans-nose-smashes-teeth-out-with-gun/

End of Watch

xcvii.   Officer Down Memorial Page. "Patrolman Gerald T DiJoseph." http://www.odmp.org/officer/4090-patrolman-gerald-t-dijoseph

Kill Supercop

xcviii.   Herszenhorn, David M. "Drug Dealer Found Guilty of Murder of Child Witness." *New York Times*, Jun 9, 2000. http://www.nytimes.com/2000/06/09/nyregion/drug-dealer-found-guilty-in-murder-of-child-witness.html

xcix.   Murphy, Mary. "Targeted by their Uniform. The Disturbing 43-Year History of Assassinations of NYPD Cops. Dec. 20 2014. http://pix11.com/2014/12/20/targeted-for-their-badge-the-disturbing-43-year-history-of-assassinations-of-nypd-cops/

c.   "The Story of Joanne Chesimard." *Law Enforcement Magazine*, May 2003. http://njlawman.com/Feature%20Pieces/Joanne%20Chesimard.htm

ci.   Murphy, Mary. "Targeted by their Uniform. The Disturbing 43-Year History of Assassinations of NYPD Cops. Dec. 20 2014. http://pix11.com/2014/12/20/targeted-for-their-badge-the-disturbing-43-year-history-of-assassinations-of-nypd-cops/

James Lancia

The Truth Hurts: Political Parties

cii.   Pavlich, Katie. "2013 Top Ten Most Dangerous Cities All Run By Democrats." *Town Hall*, Mar 12, 2014. http://townhall.com/tipsheet/katiepavlich/2014/03/12/fbi-releases-2013-most-dangerous-cities-and-theyre-all-run-by-democrats-n1807969

The Truth Hurts: White Politicians

ciii. Riger, S., Gordon, M., & Le Bailley, R. "Coping with Urban Crime: Women's use of Precautionary Behaviors." *American Journal of Community Psychology, 10.4.* 1982.

civ.   Patrick Leahy, Michael. "War on Suburbs: Obama, Julian Castro, Rev Up Affirmative Action Housing." *Breitbart*, 29 Jul. 2015, http://www.breitbart.com/big-government/2015/07/29/castro-and-obama-unite-to-subjugate-americas-suburbs-with-unlawful-affirmatively-furthering-fair-housing-rule/

cv.   Bannon, S., & Hahn, J. "Paul Ryan Betrays America: $1.1 Trillion, 2,000-Plus Page Omnibus Spending Bill Funds 'Fundamental Transformation of America'" *Breitbart*. Dec. 16, 2015. http://www.breitbart.com/big-government/2015/12/16/paul-ryan-betrays-america-1-1-trillion-2000-plus-page-omnibus-bill-funds-fundamental-transformation-america/

cvi.   Hickford, M. "White High School Students Barred from Attending Black Lives Matter Event." Mar 10, 2015. http://allenbwest.com/2015/03/white-high-school-students-barred-from-attending-black-lives-matter-event/

cvii. Operation Mockingbird, CIA Media Control Program. 2013. https://www.popularresistance.org/operation-mockingbird-cia-media-control-program/

cviii. Valentine, Douglas. "The Department of Homeland Security: When the Phoenix Comes Home to Roost." *Information Clearing House*, http://www.informationclearinghouse.info/article3225.htm

Hells Angels

cix.   Nimmo, Kurt. "Donald Trump Hit in the Pocketbook For Daring to Exercise His First Amendment Right." *Infowars*. 9 Jul. 2015. http://www.infowars.com/donald-trump-hit-in-the-pocketbook-for-daring-to-exercise-his-first-amendment-right/

Monsters Under My Bed

cx.   Golgowski, Nina. "Couple Met and Married Within a Month and Stayed Together for 65 Years…Only to be Parted After Home Invader Beat Wife To Death." *Daily Mail*, 20 Mar 2012. http://www.dailymail.co.uk/news/article-2117695/Brutal-home-invasion-Oklahoma-couple-ends-65-year-romance-meeting-blind-date.html

The Truth Hurts: The School Systems

cxi.   Conservative Tribune. "Black Teacher Makes Shocking Racist Remarks to White Special Needs Kid... Where's the Media?" 26 Jun 2015. http://conservativetribune.com/black-teacher-shocking-remarks/

cxii.   Wall, Allen. "Memo from Mexico. Who is Jose Angel Gutierrez-And What Does He Want?" Jun. 2 2004. http://www.vdare.com/articles/memo-from-mexico-by-allan-wall-175

cxiii.   Harvard Magazine, September-October 2002. http://harvardmagazine.com/2002/09/abolish-the-white-race.html

cxiv.   Ibid.

cxv.   An intelligent and well articulated review of Zinn's book is provided by Daniel J. Flynn. Flynn is the executive director of Accuracy in Academia. Article can be viewed at *George Mason University History Network*, http://historynewsnetwork.org/article/1493

cxvi.   White Genocide Project. http://whitegenocideproject.com/what-anti-whites-say/

cxvii.   Owens, Eric. "Professor Blames Baltimore Riots on 'White Privilege,' Calls for Massive Surveillance of White People." *Fox News* May 5, 2015. http://nation.foxnews.com/2015/05/05/professor-blames-baltimore-riots-white-privilege-calls-massive-surveillance-white-people

cxviii.   Flaherty, Colin. "Black Crime Claims Life of Apologist for Black Crime." *American Thinker.* Dec. 3, 2014. http://www.americanthinker.com/articles/2014/12/black_crime_claims_life_of_apologist_for_black_crime.html

cxix.   White Genocide Project. http://whitegenocideproject.com/what-anti-whites-say/

"The Man's Killing Mommy!"

cxx.   Laughland, Oliver. "Toni Morrison: I Want to See A White Man Convicted For Raping A Black Woman." *The Guardian*, 20 Apr. 2015. http://www.theguardian.com/books/2015/apr/20/toni-morrison-race-relations-america-criminal-justice-system

cxxi.   Buchanan, Patrick. "Black America's Real Problem Isn't White Racism." *Human Events*, Jul 19, 2013. http://humanevents.com/2013/07/19/black-americas-real-problem-isnt-white-racism/

cxxii.   Auster, Lawrence. "The Truth of Interracial Rape in the United States." *Front Page Mag*, May 3 2007. http://archive.frontpagemag.com/readArticle.aspx?ARTID=26368

The Truth Hurts: Protestors and Rioters

cxxiii. Extensive list at: http://www.discoverthenetworks.org/viewSubCategory.asp?id=1237

cxxiv. Human Events. "Top 10 Reasons George Soros is Dangerous. *Human Events* Apr 2, 2011. http://humanevents.com/2011/04/02/top-10-reasons-george-soros-is-dangerous/

cxxv. Shadwick, Lana. "Black Activists Call for Lynching and Hanging of White People and Cops." *Breitbart, http://www.breitbart.com/texas/2015/08/28/black-activists-called-for-lynching-and-hanging-of-white-people-and-cops/*

cxxvi. Watson, Steve. "Kill Whites and Cops": Black Lives Matter Affiliated Radio Calls for Race War." *Infowars, http://www.infowars.com/kill-whites-and-cops-black-lives-matter-affiliated-radio-show-calls-for-race-war/*

cxxvii. WECT. "NC Police Chief Out After Calling Black Lives Matter a 'terrorist' group on Facebook." http://wncn.com/2015/09/15/black-lives-matter-post-leads-to-nc-police-chiefs-retirement/

cxxviii. Burke, Jennifer. "These FBI and CDC Statistics Completely Destroy the Race Baiting, Police Bashing Narrative Out of Ferguson." *TPNN,* http://www.tpnn.com/2014/12/03/these-fbi-and-cdc-statistics-completely-destroy-the-race-baiting-police-bashing-narrative-out-of-ferguson/

"Beat That Whitey!"

cxxix. McCarthy, Peggy. "Father Panik Village: High Hopes Are Now Despair." *The New York Times*, Aug 2, 1987. http://www.nytimes.com/1987/08/02/nyregion/father-panik-village-high-hopes-are-now-despair-l-by-peggy-mccarthy.html?pagewanted=1

The Truth Hurts: Hollywood and Television

cxxx. Stein, Joel. "Who Runs Hollywood? C'mon." *Los Angeles Times*, Dec. 19, 2008. http://articles.latimes.com/2008/dec/19/opinion/oe-stein19

cxxxi. "Jamie Foxx: Great That I Get To Kill All The White People In The Movie; Praises Mixed Obama." Dec. 9, 2012. https://www.youtube.com/watch?v=Tfw-CNJbL6g

cxxxii. AM. "Oprah Winfrey: White Older People Have to Die." *Conservative Post*, Dec. 22, 2014. http://conservativepost.com/oprah-winfrey-white-older-people-have-to-die/

cxxxiii. Aamodt, M. G. "Serial Killer Statistics." Sep 6, 2014. http://maamodt.asp.radford.edu/serial killer information center/project description.htm

The Truth Hurts: The Ugly Face Behind the Hate and White Genocide

cxxxiv. Kapner, Nathanael. "Fact Sheet: Jews Control America." *Real Jew News.* May 23, 2013. http://www.re-aljewnews.com/?p=82134

cxxxv. Preston, James PhD. "Shockwaves Part III," *Veterans Today*, Mar. 12, 2015. http://www.veteranstoday.com/2015/03/12/shockwaves-part-iii/

cxxxvi. IAP News. "Sharon to Peres: 'Don't Worry About American Pressure, We Control America'" *Washington Report on Middle East Affairs*, 3 Oct. 2001. http://www.wrmea.org/old-html/sharon-to-peres-don-t-worry-about-american-pressure-we-control-america.html

cxxxvii. Anders. "Inverted Racism: Unpunished Jewish/Muslim Desire to Exterminate White Race-By Genocide and Multiculture." *New.Euro-Med.DK*, Sep. 20, 2015. http://new.euro-med.dk/20150920-inverted-racism-unpunished-jewishmuslim-desire-to-exterminate-white-race-by-genocide-and-multiculture.php

cxxxviii. *Israel Elect.* http://israelect.com/ChildrenOfYahweh/Other%20Reading/greetings.htm

cxxxix. Hunt, Kyle. "The Jewish Jihad Against the Western World and the Coming Crusade." *Renegade Tribune*, Sep 3, 2015. http://renegadetribune.com/the-jewish-jihad-against-europeans-and-the-coming-crusade/

Gangland

cxl. Abrams, Floyd. "*Speaking Freely: Trials of the First Amendment.*" New York, NY: Penguin Books. 2006.

The Truth Hurts: So Called Black Leaders and Politicians

cxli. Goldberg, Bernard. "What President Obama Left Out of his Talk on Race." Jul. 21, 2013. http://bernardgoldberg.com/what-president-obama-left-out-of-his-talk-on-race/

cxlii. Key, Pam. "Farrakhan: We Must Rise Up and Kill Those Who Kill Us; Stalk Them and Kill Them. *Breitbart.* 4 Aug. 2015, *http://www.breitbart.com/video/2015/08/04/farrakhan-we-must-rise-up-and-kill-those-who-kill-us-stalk-them-and-kill-them/*

cxliii. Snyder, Michael. "It's Official: Police Were Ordered to Stand Down and Let the Baltimore Riots Rage Out of Control." *Infowars*, 1 May, 2015, *http://www.infowars.com/its-official-police-were-ordered-to-stand-down-and-let-the-baltimore-riots-rage-out-of-control/*

cxliv.   Daniels, Kit. "Breaking: Baltimore Mayor Key Player in Obama's Federal Takeover of Local Police. Mayor's Link to Justice Dept. Explains Why She Gave Rioters 'Space to Destroy.'" *Infowars. Apr. 28, 2015,* http://www.infowars.com/breaking-baltimore-mayor-key-player-in-obamas-federal-takeover-of-local-police/

cxlv.   *Time.* May 1, 2015. http://time.com/3843870/marilyn-mosby-transcript-freddie-gray/

cxlvi.   Farrell, Keith. "Racial Double Standard: Black Unemployment Under Barack Obama." *The Federalist Papers Project, http://www.thefederalistpapers.org/us/racial-double-standard-black-unemployment-under-barack-obama*

cxlvii.   It is very difficult to obtain exact data of murder rates in South Africa as the corrupt government does not accurately document race of suspects and victims. Excellent articles with data statistics available at *UnPoliticallyCorrect.* Dec. 7, 2013. https://unpoliticallycorrect2016.wordpress.com/category/black-on-white-crimes/

The Truth Hurts: Gun Control Advocates

cxlviii.   "Jacob Zuma Sings 'Kill the Boer' at ANC Centenery Celebrations in Bloemfontein, South Africa" *YouTube,* Published Mar. 14, 2012. https://www.youtube.com/watch?v=6fzRSE_p1Ys

cxlix.   Site with statistics drawn from the Chicago Sun Times, Homicide Watch Chicago, The Chicago Tribune, Chicago Redeye Homicide Tracker and more at: http://heyjackass.com/category/2014-chicago-crime-murder-stats/

cl.   Madhani, Aamer. "Chicago Records 51 Homicides in January, Highest Toll Since 2000." Feb 1, 2016. http://www.usatoday.com/story/news/2016/02/01/chicago-records-51-homicides-january-highest-toll-since-2000/79632136/

cli.   Hawkins, Awr. "Report: 92 Percent of Mass Shootings Since 2009 Occurred in Gun Free Zones." *Breitbart,* Oct 11, 2014. http://www.breitbart.com/big-government/2014/10/11/report-92-percent-of-mass-shootings-since-2009-occured-in-gun-free-zones/

clii.   CNN Staff. "Study: Gun Homicides, Violence Down Sharply in the Past 20 Years." *CNN,* May 9, 2013. http://www.cnn.com/2013/05/08/us/study-gun-homicide/

cliii.   Ibid.

cliv.   UNODA. "UNODA's Mandate on Regional Disarmament." http://www.un.org/disarmament/disarmsec/about/

clv.   Hoft, Jim. "Gun Crime Soars in England Where Guns are Banned." 15 Dec. 2012. http://humanevents.com/2012/12/15/gun-crime-soars-in-england-by-35-where-guns-are-banned/

clvi. Roberts, Dan. "Every Mass Shooting Shares One Thing In Common & It's Not Weapons." *Ammoland*, Apr. 1, 2013. http://www.ammoland.com/2013/04/every-mass-shooting-in-the-last-20-years-shares-psychotropic-drugs/#axzz3dzLdQso4

clvii. Jacobson, Brad. "Obama Received 20 Million from Healthcare Industry in 2008 Campaign." *Common Dreams*, Jan 12, 2010. http://www.commondreams.org/news/2010/01/12/obama-received-20-million-healthcare-industry-2008-campaign

End of an Era

clviii. Jaffe, Alexandra. "Huckabee: 'Michael Brown Acted Like a Thug'" *CNN Politics*, Dec. 3, 2014. http://www.cnn.com/2014/12/03/politics/ferguson-mike-huckabee-michael-brown-shooting-thug/

ABOUT THE AUTHOR

James Lancia is a retired police officer who worked closely with the FBI, DEA, ATF, and Statewide Narcotics Agency in Connecticut. As a patrolman and while a member of the Bridgeport Police Department's elite units-Tactical, Special Services, and Anti Crime Divisions- he patrolled the streets during the country's high-crime crack epidemic. The many dangerous neighborhoods on his beat included the sixth largest housing project in the nation, Father Panic Village, which was rated the worst in the country according to FBI statistics.

Since retiring, he has used his skills in boxing, kickboxing, and weightlifting to train boxers and for a short time, along with a former colleague, he worked closely with Kevin Rooney, former trainer of world champion Mike Tyson.

He is now a military artist, painting museum pieces for the French Foreign Legion. His work has been featured in the French Foreign Legion Headquarters Museum in Aubagne, France. His historical military artwork has also been featured at West Point and in various other US museums and magazines.